RUSSIAN ENGAGEMENT IN THE WESTERN HEMISPHERE

HEARING

BEFORE THE

SUBCOMMITTEE ON
THE WESTERN HEMISPHERE

OF THE

COMMITTEE ON FOREIGN AFFAIRS
HOUSE OF REPRESENTATIVES

ONE HUNDRED FOURTEENTH CONGRESS

FIRST SESSION

OCTOBER 22, 2015

Serial No. 114–110

Printed for the use of the Committee on Foreign Affairs

Available via the World Wide Web: http://www.foreignaffairs.house.gov/ or
http://www.gpo.gov/fdsys/

U.S. GOVERNMENT PUBLISHING OFFICE

97–266PDF   WASHINGTON : 2015

COMMITTEE ON FOREIGN AFFAIRS

EDWARD R. ROYCE, California, *Chairman*

CHRISTOPHER H. SMITH, New Jersey
ILEANA ROS-LEHTINEN, Florida
DANA ROHRABACHER, California
STEVE CHABOT, Ohio
JOE WILSON, South Carolina
MICHAEL T. McCAUL, Texas
TED POE, Texas
MATT SALMON, Arizona
DARRELL E. ISSA, California
TOM MARINO, Pennsylvania
JEFF DUNCAN, South Carolina
MO BROOKS, Alabama
PAUL COOK, California
RANDY K. WEBER SR., Texas
SCOTT PERRY, Pennsylvania
RON DeSANTIS, Florida
MARK MEADOWS, North Carolina
TED S. YOHO, Florida
CURT CLAWSON, Florida
SCOTT DesJARLAIS, Tennessee
REID J. RIBBLE, Wisconsin
DAVID A. TROTT, Michigan
LEE M. ZELDIN, New York
DANIEL DONOVAN, New York

ELIOT L. ENGEL, New York
BRAD SHERMAN, California
GREGORY W. MEEKS, New York
ALBIO SIRES, New Jersey
GERALD E. CONNOLLY, Virginia
THEODORE E. DEUTCH, Florida
BRIAN HIGGINS, New York
KAREN BASS, California
WILLIAM KEATING, Massachusetts
DAVID CICILLINE, Rhode Island
ALAN GRAYSON, Florida
AMI BERA, California
ALAN S. LOWENTHAL, California
GRACE MENG, New York
LOIS FRANKEL, Florida
TULSI GABBARD, Hawaii
JOAQUIN CASTRO, Texas
ROBIN L. KELLY, Illinois
BRENDAN F. BOYLE, Pennsylvania

AMY PORTER, *Chief of Staff*   THOMAS SHEEHY, *Staff Director*
JASON STEINBAUM, *Democratic Staff Director*

————

SUBCOMMITTEE ON THE WESTERN HEMISPHERE

JEFF DUNCAN, South Carolina, *Chairman*

CHRISTOPHER H. SMITH, New Jersey
ILEANA ROS-LEHTINEN, Florida
MICHAEL T. McCAUL, Texas
MATT SALMON, Arizona
RON DeSANTIS, Florida
TED S. YOHO, Florida
DANIEL DONOVAN, New York

ALBIO SIRES, New Jersey
JOAQUIN CASTRO, Texas
ROBIN L. KELLY, Illinois
GREGORY W. MEEKS, New York
ALAN GRAYSON, Florida
ALAN S. LOWENTHAL, California

CONTENTS

RUSSIAN ENGAGEMENT IN THE WESTERN HEMISPHERE

THURSDAY, OCTOBER 22, 2015

House of Representatives,
Subcommittee on the Western Hemisphere,
Committee on Foreign Affairs,
Washington, DC.

The committee met, pursuant to notice, at 2 o'clock p.m., in room 2172 Rayburn House Office Building, Hon. Jeff Duncan (chairman of the subcommittee) presiding.

Mr. DUNCAN. A quorum being present, the subcommittee will come to order. I now would like to recognize myself for an opening statement.

This subcommittee hearing is the third in a series of hearings that we have held to examine the presence and activities of certain countries operating here in the Western Hemisphere. In February, we looked at Iran and Hezbollah's presence in the region, the failure of the State Department to prioritize these actors in view of a potential Iran nuclear deal and the limited U.S. intelligence capabilities focused on these issues.

In July, we examined China's extensive engagement with the region through trade and the investment of hundreds of billions of dollars, energy cooperation, infrastructure projects and a range of security activities including satellite cooperation, arms sales, and military exchanges.

So today we will meet to consider Russia's engagement in Latin America and Caribbean. Following the Cold War, Russia began taking more of a pronounced interest in the region especially during the 2008 crisis in Georgia. When the U.S. responded to Russia's aggression in Georgia by sending naval forces to the Black Sea, Russia deployed nuclear-capable bombers to the Caribbean and a four-ship naval flotilla to conduct military exercises with the Venezuelan navy and make port calls in Cuba and Nicaragua.

Let there be light.

Russia also stepped up its diplomatic outreach with a visit to the region from then-President Medvedev, and subsequent visits from the Presidents of Venezuela, Nicaragua, Bolivia and Ecuador to Moscow. Following Russia's invasion of the Ukraine in 2014, Russia again ushered in another wave of military and diplomatic activities with particular emphasis on anti-American and undemocratic countries, those with close proximity to U.S. borders, or those with unique capabilities of interest to Russia.

Last year proved a very eventful year for Russia in the Western Hemisphere. Reportedly, Russia began talks on Nicaragua, Cuba and Venezuela about establishing bases for resupplying Russian warships and potentially refueling Russian long-range bombers. In April, the U.S. observed two Russian ships operating in waters close to Cuba near the U.S. naval station in Mayport, Florida. That same month, the Russian foreign minister visited Nicaragua, Cuba, Peru and Chile.

In June, NORAD reported it had scrambled two F–22s and two F–15s after seeing a fleet of Russian bombers off the coast of Alaska and California. In July, Russian President Putin traveled in the region to visit Cuba, Nicaragua, Argentina and Brazil. At that time, Russia forgave 90 percent of Cuba's debt, and reportedly Russia and Cuba agreed to reopen the Lourdes base only 150 miles from the United States coast.

End of September, U.S. intercepted Russia fighter jets and tankers in airspace near Alaska, and just in November of last year, Russia announced that it had planned to send its long-range bombers to the Gulf of Mexico and the Caribbean. The United States did very little in response to all these developments.

Subsequently, this past January, Russia sent a ship to Cuba on the eve of Assistant Secretary Roberta Jacobsen's visit. This was followed by a visit from the Russian foreign minister to Cuba, Nicaragua and Venezuela in February, and a visit from the Russian defense minister to Cuba, Colombia, Nicaragua and Guatemala in March.

Most recently, as Russia has deepened its military efforts in Syria, reportedly Cuban troops have been sent to Syria to operate Russian tanks. Such Russian overreach in its own region, in the Middle East, and now in the Western Hemisphere does not send a positive message to the United States and our freedom-loving allies. Indeed, in view of Russia's aggression in its own neighborhood, violations of arms control treaties, cyberattacks on U.S. infrastructure, and continued partnerships with Iran, Syria, Cuba and Venezuela, Russian actions do not signal an interest in peace nor of global stability.

In the Western Hemisphere, Russia's engagement appears driven primarily by geopolitical and security considerations rather than solely economic interest. After all, in 2013, Russia's bilateral trade with the region was only $18 billion, 14 times less than China's trade with the region.

In contrast, from 2001 to 2013, Russia sold Latin America almost $15 billion in arms which amounts to 40 percent of the arms purchased by the region from external actors. Similarly, from 2008 to 2011, Russia sold more than 3,000 surface-to-air missiles to the region, and multiple countries also have Russian helicopters.

Beyond arms sales Russia has sought positions of influence. Reportedly, Ecuador, Nicaragua, Bolivia and Argentina have all granted Russia access to their airspace and ports. Russia's only transoceanic shipping line to South America runs from Russia to Ecuador, and multiple countries have agreed to or are considering participating in Russia's GLONASS satellite navigation system. Furthermore, Russia seems to have prioritized relations with countries close to U.S. borders. Russia has provided armored vehicles, aircraft missiles and helicopters to Mexico, and assistance in Mexico's fight against criminal organizations.

Several of El Salvador's leaders received training in the Soviet Union, and Nicaragua has agreed to host a new Russian counterdrug center, Russian munitions disposal plant, and a 130 Russian counternarcotics trainers who conduct joint patrols with the Nicaraguans. In addition, Russia has cultivated a strategic alliance with Brazil and a strategic partnership with Argentina as Russia's top two trading partners. Furthermore, Russian engagement in Peru has resulted in strong military ties with that country, counterdrug cooperation, and reportedly the planning and executing of joint strategic operations.

Today, Venezuela remains a key linchpin for Russia activity in Latin America, and in return Russia has provided Venezuela with arms sales, a $2 billion loan, and energy cooperation in the Orinoco River Basin.

In conclusion, Russia's engagement in the Western Hemisphere is deeply troubling. At a time when Russia is flexing its geopolitical muscles in other parts of the world, its power projection in our very region should be met with U.S. strength, resilience and clarity. In 2009, President Putin called cooperation with Latin American states one of the key and very promising lines of Russian foreign policy. The United States should recognize this and adapt accordingly in our response.

So I will look forward to hearing from the expert panelists on this topic. And I want to just emphasize that this is just a series of hearings that we are having focused on not only the involvement of other countries in this hemisphere, but I want to emphasize the lack of U.S. engagement in this hemisphere, and so I would love for the panelists to touch on that as well.

With that I will turn to the ranking member Mr. Sires for his opening statement.

Mr. SIRES. Thank you, Mr. Chairman. Good afternoon. Thank you for our witnesses for being here today.

Today we are examining Russia's engagement in Latin America and the Caribbean. Russia has been involved in Latin America since its support for Cuba and Nicaragua during the Cold War. The post-Cold War era saw a decline in Russian engagement, but as Russia-U.S. relations have become tenser in recent years, Putin is reviving these old ties to the Western Hemisphere. Russia has had a series of high profile state visits, proposed investment and most important an increase in military sales and military exercise in the region.

According to General John F. Kelly, commander of the U.S. Southern Command, Russia has courted Cuba, Venezuela and Nicaragua to gain access to airbases and ports for resupply of Russian naval assets and strategic bombers operating in the Western Hemisphere. Putin's high level visit included travel to Cuba, Nicaragua, Argentina and Brazil, while the Russian prime minister has also made trips to Cuba and Nicaragua.

Russia's interests in the region are to increase military cooperation, find new partners in the wake of U.S. and EU sanctions on Russia's economy, and try and promote the perception that they are a global power. Though these high level visits and proposed agreements are just for the Russian investment in the region, experts doubt Russia's ability to fulfill its economic commitment.

What concerns me is Russia's continued arms sales to the region, especially on the heels of their support for ruthless dictators like Syria's Bashir al-Assad. Now we are seeing reports of the Cuban military on the ground in Syria assisting Russia in bombing innocent civilians and moderate anti-government forces.

For too many years the United States has focused on other parts of the world which has led to the neglect of our neighborhood. We must remain vigilant on what the long-term consequences might be and reaffirm our own commitment to the region. And I look forward to hearing from our panelists today. Thank you.

Mr. DUNCAN. Wow. That was a short opening statement.

Mr. SIRES. I want to hear what they have got to say.

Mr. DUNCAN. I appreciate the ranking member. I do as well. The bios are in your binders and so I won't do the bios. I will just start with recognizing each member will have 5 minutes. There is a light system, so when it gets close to running out of time you will have yellow and then red, and then if you could wrap it up when the red light comes on.

So Douglas Farah, welcome back. You have been a great panelist in the past and a tremendous asset for me. I have learned a lot from you. I look forward to learning more from you today. You are recognized for 5 minutes.

STATEMENT OF MR. DOUG FARAH, PRESIDENT, IBI CONSULTANTS

Mr. FARAH. Thank you, Chairman Duncan, I appreciate your kind words. And thank you, Ranking Member Sires and members of the committee for the opportunity to discuss Russia's——

Mr. DUNCAN. Now if you could pull that microphone just a little closer. We are recording this and I want to make sure we get it all. So thank you.

Mr. FARAH. Is that better? Okay, thank you.

Over the past 3 years, as you have noted, President Putin has made no secret of his desire to create a multipolar world where the United States is not dominant. Leaders of the U.S. defense and intelligence communities have responded to Russia's growing global assertiveness by singling out Russia as the primary military and strategic threat to the United States, particularly following Russia's annexation of the Crimea and other hostile activities. However, that threat assessment is seldom applied to Latin America. Yet, given its current positioning one could argue that Russia now has more influence in Latin America than ever before, even including the height of the Cold War.

This will likely remain true despite the recent announcement of the normalization of diplomatic relations between Cuba and the United States. During most of the Cold War, the Soviet Union's only reliable ally in Latin America was Cuba, which in turn helped sponsor insurgent movements across the hemisphere. With the 1979 triumph of the Sandinista Revolution, the Kremlin gained a second state partner, but when the Berlin Wall fell 12 years later, Russia's regional influence ebbed to almost nothing.

But since 2005, riding the wave of radical anti-U.S. populism sponsored by the late President Hugo Chavez of Venezuela, Russia is now firmly allied with the ranks of Latin America's populist, authoritarian and strongly anti-American leaders of the Bolivarian Alliance bloc known as ALBA. The Putin government is providing all the nations with weapons, police and military training and equipment, intelligence technology and training, nuclear technology, oil exploration equipment, financial assistance, and an influential friend in the United Nations Security Council and other international forums. With Russia's help the once shared hemispheric values of functioning and democratic systems are being replaced by a toxic mix of anti-democratic values, massive corruption, and a doctrine that draws on totalitarian models.

The ALBA bloc embraces terrorism and terrorist groups such as the FARC in Colombia, Hezbollah, and the Spanish ETA and its military doctrine includes the justification of the use of weapons of mass destruction against the United States. In return, these allies are shielding Russia from international isolation, providing political and diplomatic support, and opening access to financial markets for sanctioned Russian banks and companies.

Russia has also helped create an important regional media and social media network offering coordinated messages of unstinting support for Putin while casting the United States as the global aggressor. At the same time, ALBA countries are increasing Russia's military access to the hemisphere's ports and airspace and ultimately increasing Russia's sphere of influence in a region where the United States has seldom been so directly challenged.

As noted in his July visit, President Putin made multiple gifts to his friends in the region, including the forgiveness of Cuban debt, declaring a strategic alliance with Argentina, and discussing nuclear energy agreements over dinner with Argentine President Cristina Fernandez de Kirchner. Putin also promised President Daniel Ortega of Nicaragua Russia's military protection for the canal which will likely never be completed, but would provide Russia with coveted deep sea seaports.

It is worth noting that with the establishment of these strategic alliances, delegations of senior Russian military and foreign relations officials routinely travel through the region, including individuals under sanctions by the United States and the European Union. As noted, General Kelly is aware of this issue and has said that over the past three decades, ''It has been over three decades since we last saw this type of high profile Russian presence in Latin America.'' He added that under Putin we have seen a clear return to the Cold War tactics.

It is not that the nature of the Russian state is not understood. In March 2015, Director of National Intelligence James Clapper labeled Russia a ''threat actor'' and an example of a nation where ''the nexus among organized crime, state actors, and business blurs the distinction between state policy and private gain.''

While one can observe the accuracy of this assessment of Russia's intentions and capability in many parts of the world, the growing mixture of Russian state presence, business ventures, soft power overtures, criminal activity and proxy activities in Latin America have gone largely unexamined. One repeat visitor to Latin

America who provides a particularly useful lens to understand Russian activities in the region is General Valery Gerasimov, chief of staff of the Russian Federation and chief architect of the Gerasimov Doctrine. The influential doctrine posits that the rules of war have changed and that there is a ''blurring of the lines between war and peace.'' He advocates an asymmetrical series of actions in a permanently operating front through an entire territory of the enemy state.

This is the prism through which the Russian's engagement in Latin America should be viewed. This is how and why Russia is engaging with select Latin America states. If you look closely at what they are doing they are focusing on four distinct areas. As noted, the sale of weapons; also police, military and intelligence assistance; access to financial institutions, which I detail in my written testimony at some length; and creating this counter-narrative which I talked about before where the United States is constantly portrayed as the aggressor and Russia as an alternative to that.

In addition, IBI Consultants research has mapped out an interesting and opaque network of former senior military and KGB officials operating in Central America. This network deserves extensive more research. Russia's rise underscores, as Chairman Duncan said, the significant loss of Washington's ability to shape events in a region close to home and of significant strategic interest. While the U.S. position remains preeminent due to geographic proximity, cultural ties and trade ties, it is eroding more quickly than is often understood.

In a time of resource scarcity, Russia has managed to leverage a small amount of resources into significant gain. The Russia agenda is aided and abetted by the ALBA bloc of nations in which there is no independent media and where the official media magnifies each statement and donation. The United States needs a much more visible return to the region to counter the perception and the reality that Russia is again a major strategic influence in the region. Thank you.

[The prepared statement of Mr. Farah follows:]

Testimony of Douglas Farah
President, IBI Consultants, LLC

Before the House Committee on Foreign Affairs Subcommittee on the Western
Hemisphere

Russia's Engagement in the Western Hemisphere

October 22, 2015
2172 Rayburn House Office Building

Chairman Duncan, Ranking Member Sires and members of the committee, thank you for the opportunity to discuss Russia's strategic engagement in the Western Hemisphere and the implications for U.S. policy in the region. I speak only for IBI Consultants and not for any other institution with which I am affiliated. Much of the research used in this testimony is the result of the work of my co-workers Thomas Ewing and Liana Eustacia Reyes.

Over the past three years Russian President Vladimir Putin has made no secret of his desire to restore Russia to superpower status to create a multi-polar world where the United States is not dominant. Leaders of the U.S. defense and intelligence communities have responded to Russia's growing global assertiveness by singling out Russia as the primary military and strategic threat to the United States, particularly following Russia's recent annexation of Crimea and hostile activities in the Ukraine and Syria. However, that threat assessment is seldom applied to Latin America.

Yet given its current positioning, one could argue that Russia now has more influence in Latin America than ever before, even including at the height of the Cold War. This will likely remain true despite the recent announcement of the normalization of diplomatic relations between Cuba and the United States and Russia's ongoing economic turmoil.

During most of the Cold War, the Soviet Union's only reliable ally in Latin America was Cuba, which in turn helped sponsor insurgent movements across the hemisphere. With the 1979 triumph of the Sandinista revolution in Nicaragua, the Kremlin gained a second state partner. But when the Berlin Wall fell 12 years later, Russia's regional influence ebbed to almost nothing in Latin America.

But since 2005, riding on the wave of radical anti-U.S. populism sponsored by Hugo Chávez in Venezuela, Russia is now firmly allied with the ranks of Latin America's populist, authoritarian and virulently anti-American leaders of the Bolivarian Alliance for the Peoples of Our America – (*Alianza Bolivariana para los Pueblos de Nuestra América* – ALBA).[1]

The Putin government is providing ALBA nations with weapons, police and military training and equipment, intelligence technology and training, nuclear technology, oil exploration equipment, financial assistance, and an influential friend on the United Nations Security Council and other international forums.

With Russia's help and advise the once-shared hemispheric values of a functioning democratic system are being replaced by a toxic mix of anti-democratic values, massive corruption, and a doctrine that draws on totalitarian models. The ALBA bloc embraces terrorism and terrorist groups such as the FARC in Colombia, Hezbollah and the Spanish ETA and its military doctrine includes the justification for the use of weapons of mass destruction against the United States.

---

[1] Members of ALBA include Venezuela, Bolivia, Ecuador, Nicaragua, El Salvador, Suriname and several Caribbean islands. Argentina, while not formally a member of the organization, sponsors ALBA events and behaves a member of the alliance, including increasing aggressive attacks on the United States.

Russia, eager to strengthen these governments, now has at least seven unconditional allies in the region,[2] most of them among the least democratic and most repressive in the hemisphere. During the past two years Russia has expanded its dealings with these nations at a rapid pace.

In return, these allies are shielding Russia from international isolation, providing political and diplomatic support, and opening access to financial markets for sanctions Russian banks and companies.

Russia has also helped create an important regional media and social media network consisting of a host of state sponsored websites, government-owned traditional media and a significant Twitter presence of several presidents. This network offers coordinated messages of unstinting support for Putin while casting the United States as the global aggressor.[3] At the same time, ALBA countries are increasing Russia's military access to the hemisphere's ports and airspace, and ultimately, increasing Russia's sphere of influence in a region where the United States has seldom been so directly challenged.

In a high-profile visit to the region in July 2014, Putin offered multiple gifts to his friends. He forgave some $30 billion, or 90%, of Cuba's unpaid Soviet debt, noted as a possible concession to reestablish the Lourdes listening post facility on the island to bolster Russia's electronic spying capabilities close to the United States.[4]

Additionally, Putin declared a "strategic alliance" with Argentina and discussed satellite and nuclear energy agreements over dinner with Argentine President Cristina Fernandez de Kirchner. He also promised full support in Brazil for a new BRIC[5] bloc international lending institution to counter the World Bank. And, in a surprise visit to Nicaragua, Putin promised President, Daniel Ortega, Russia's military protection for Nicaragua's new ambitious multi-billion dollar canal project. In addition to Nicaragua's canal project – which is unlikely ever to be completed but could provide Russia with coveted deep sea ports in the hemisphere – Russia is also providing assistance with the development of a regional counter-narcotics and police-training center, named after Marshal of the Soviet Union, Georgy Zhukov, which has been created to displace U.S. counter-narcotics efforts in the hemisphere.

It is worth noting that throughout these agreements and establishment of these strategic alliances, delegations of senior Russian military and foreign relations officials routinely

---

[2] These include the Bolivarian bloc of nations (Venezuela, Bolivia, Ecuador, Nicaragua Cuba and El Salvador) as well as Argentina.

[3] See: Douglas Farah, "The Advance of Radical Populist Doctrine in Latin America: How the Bolivarian Alliance is Remaking Militaries, Dismantling Democracy and Combatting the Empire," PRISM, Center for Complex Operations, National Defense University, Summer 2015, accessed at: http://cco.ndu.edu/Portals/96/Documents/prism/prism 5-3/The Advance Of Radical Populist Doctrine in Latin America.pdf

[4] Alex Luhn, "Russia to reopen spy base in Cuba as relations with U.S. continue to sour," The Guardian (July 16, 2014), accessed at: http://www.theguardian.com/world/2014/jul/16/russia-reopening-spy-base-cuba-us-relations-sour

[5] The BRIC bloc is composed of Brazil, Russia, India, and China.

travel through the region, including several leaders under sanctions by the United States and European Union for Russia's recent actions in Crimea and Ukraine.[6]

As General John Kelly, commander of the U.S. Southern Command (SOUTHCOM) noted in recent Congressional testimony, "it has been over three decades since we last saw this type of high-profile Russian presence" in Latin America."[7] In his command's 2015 Posture Statement Kelly added that

> Periodically since 2008, Russia has pursued an increased presence in Latin America through propaganda, military arms and equipment sales, counterdrug agreements, and trade. Under President Putin, however, we have seen a clear return to Cold War-tactics. As part of its global strategy, Russia is using power projection in an attempt to erode U.S. leadership and challenge U.S. influence in the Western Hemisphere. While these actions do not pose an immediate threat, Russia's activities in the hemisphere are concerning and underscore the importance of remaining engaged with our partners.[8]

While General Kelly is correct in noting that Russia in Latin America does not yet present an imminent military threat to the United States, Russian officials have been open and explicit about the desire to confront the United States in its main sphere of influence in order to counter what they perceive to be U.S. interference in Russia's border territories. In the current context of Latin America, it is clear the Russians have made greater strides toward their goals than is usually acknowledged.

It is not that the nature of the Russian state is not known or understood. In March 2015, Director of National Intelligence James R. Clapper labeled Russia a "threat actor" and an example of a nation where "the nexus among organized crime, state actors, and business blurs the distinction between state policy and private gain."[9] The 2015 National Military Strategy presented by the Joint Chiefs of Staff noted that Russia "has repeatedly demonstrated that it does not respect the sovereignty of its neighbors and it is willing to use force to achieve its goals. Russia's military actions are undermining regional security directly and through proxy forces."[10]

---

[6] These include Viktor Ivanov, head of Russia's Federal Drug Control Service, who attended the inauguration of the school in Nicaragua; Igor Sechin, head of the Russian oil giant Rosneft and former deputy prime minister; and Valery Gerasimov, chief of staff of the Russian army.

[7] Kristina Wong, "Putin's quiet Latin America play," The Hill, March 21, 2014, accessed at: http://thehill.com/policy/defense/201305-putins-quiet-play-for-latin-america

[8] Gen. John F. Kelly, "Posture Statement of General John R. Kelly, United States Marine Corps, Commander, United States Southern Command Before the 114th Congress Senate Armed Services Committee," March 12, 2015, accessed at: http://www.southcom.mil/newsroom/Documents/SOUTHCOM_POSTURE_STATEMENT_FINAL_201 5.pdf

[9] James R. Clapper. Director of National Intelligence, "Statement for the Record: Worldwide Threat Assessment of the U.S. Intelligence Community," House Appropriations Subcommittee on Defense, March 25, 2015, accessed at: http://docs.house.gov/meetings/AP/AP02/20150325/103200/HHRG-114-AP02-Wstate-ClapperJ-20150325.pdf

[10] "The National Military Strategy of the United States of America 2015," June 2015, accessed at: http://www.jcs.mil/Portals/36/Documents/Publications/2015_National_Military_Strategy.pdf

While one can observe the accuracy of the assessments of Russian intentions and capabilities in many parts of the world, the burgeoning mixture of Russian state presence, business ventures, soft power overtures, criminal activity and proxy activities in Latin America – and particularly Central America – have gone largely unexamined. Yet the hemisphere and isthmus of strategic interest to the United States has been an area of intense Russian state activities.

The most tangible signs of Russia's growing interest and footprint are the constant visits to the hemisphere and Central American by senior Russian political and military figures, including: Putin in 2014; and multiple visits in the past two years by Defense Minister Shoigu; Foreign Minister Sergey Lavrov; Counter-narcotics chief Viktor Ivanov; Prime Minister Dmitry Medvdev; and other senior officials.[11]

Where the Russian state establishes a presence, Russian organized crime invariably follows. The immediate consequence is the rapid increase in cocaine flows from Latin America to Russia, and the former Soviet Union, with almost all of the cocaine that is shipped to originating from countries that Russia vehemently supports – Venezuela, Nicaragua, and Ecuador. Regional law enforcement officials in Central America and Colombia say there is a noticeable increase in Russian organized crime activity in Central America, primarily in cocaine trafficking via the Pacific Coast. Among the groups identified as trafficking via shipping containers are the Solntsevskaya Brotherhood and the Brother's Circle, the latter considered a top tier TOC group with close ties to the Russian state.[12]

One of the repeat visitors to Latin America who provides a particularly useful lens to understand Russian activities in the region is Gen. Valery Gerosimov, chief of staff of the Russian Federation and architect of the Gerosimov Doctrine. The influential Russian doctrine posits that the rules of war have changed, there is a "blurring of the lines between war and peace," and "nonmilitary means of achieving military and strategic goals has grown and, in many cases exceeded the power of weapons in their effectiveness." He advocates for asymmetrical actions that combine the use of special forces, information warfare that create "a permanently operating front through the entire territory of the enemy state."[13]

This is the prism through which Russian engagement in Latin America should be viewed. All of the main elements of the doctrine are being carried out in Latin America. This is how and why Russia is engaging with select Latin American states.

How is Russia doing this? As many observers have noted, Russia does not have the financial wherewithal in a time of economic crisis to match what the former Soviet Union could offer.

---

[11] For a comprehensive look at Russia's engagement on a state by state basis in Latin America and the high-level visits see: R Evan Ellis, "The New Russian Engagement wit Latin America: Strategic Position, Commerce, and Dreams of the Past," U.S. Army War College, Strategic Studies Institute, June 17, 2015, accessed at: http://www.strategicstudiesinstitute.army.mil/pubs/display.cfm?pubID=1275

[12] Farah interviews with U.S., Colombian, European and Central American law enforcement officials and diplomats, January to June 2015.

[13] Gen. Valery Gerosimov, "The Value of Science in Prediction," Military-Industrial Kurier, February 27, 2013, accessed at: https://inmoscowsshadows.wordpress.com/2014/07/06/the-gerasimov-doctrine-and-russian-non-linear-war/

And it is clear that many of the mega projects it has embraced around the region simply never come to fruition. But a more careful examination of Russian activities shows there are four main areas where it has leveraged its relatively small amount of resources to some effect within the overarching Gerosimov doctrine.

These include:

> The sale of weapons: In addition to the hundreds of thousands of the newest model AK-47 assault rifles, Russian weapons sales include tanks, helicopters, supersonic combat aircraft, and surface-to-air missiles. After registering no sales of surface-to-air missiles to Latin America during most of the past decade, Russia sold more than 3,000 to the region from 2008-2011.[14] Russia's primary client of these weapons is Venezuela, which was ranked 5th largest recipient of arms deliveries from Russia in 2011 at an estimated worth of 1.7 billion.[15] Argentina and other nations are promising to follow suit. Chavez's government secured a $2.2 billion loan in 2010 to purchase a large batch of Russian weapons for its army, including 92 T-72M1M main battle tanks, about 240 BMP 3 fighting vehicles and BTR-80 armored personnel carriers, and a variety of artillery systems. In total, it is estimated that Venezuela's arms transfer agreements with Russia amount to $13.1 billion, noting a 52 percent increase between 2007 and 2011.[16]

> Police, military and intelligence assistance: The Russian push includes the creation of the Marshal of the Soviet Union Greorgy Zhukov regional counter-narcotics training center in Nicaragua, along with a non-public agreement for a permanent presence of 130 Russian counter-narcotics trainers, who frequently conduct joint patrols with their Nicaragua counterparts.[17] In addition, the Russians have built a munitions disposal plant and have promised to build a $14 million new military hospital.[18] Russia is also now offering an almost unlimited amount of scholarships for regional military, police and intelligence officials, as well as providing friendly governments with new, much more sophisticated electronic surveillance equipment and other intelligence equipment.[19]

---

[14] Richard F. Grimmett and Paul k. Kerr, "Conventional Arms Transfers to Developing Nations 2004-2011)," CRS R42678 (Aug 24, 2012), accessed at: http://fas.org/sgp/crs/weapons/R42678.pdf p. 67, which notes that Russia has sold 3000 more surface-to-air missiles to Venezuela than any other country in the world.

[15] 1-4 were Saudi Arabia, India, Pakistan, and the U.A.E.
http://fas.org/sgp/crs/weapons/R42678.pdf

[16] Richard F. Grimmett and Paul k. Kerr, "Conventional Arms Transfers to Developing Nations 2004-2011)," CRS R42678 (Aug 24, 2012); accessed at http://fas.org/sgp/crs/weapons/R42678.pdf

[17] For further information on the training center see: "Russia-Nicaragua: multifaceted cooperation," The Voice of Russia, April 22, 2013, accessed at:
http://sputniknews.com/voiceofrussia/2013_04_22/Russia-Nicaragua-multifaceted-cooperation/ . The agreement on allowing the permanent presence of 130 trainers is in possession of the author.

[18] The munitions plant is to both get rid of old munitions that are dangerous and reactivate some munitions to "avoid the expense" of purchasing new ordinance. See: "Top Russian military brass visits Nicaragua," Nicaragua Dispatch, April 22, 2013, accessed at:
http://nicaraguadispatch.com/2013/04/top-russian-military-brass-visits-nicaragua/

[19] Farah interviews in Nicaragua and El Salvador, January to June 2015.

➢ Access for financial institutions: Russian bankers have long pushed for greater access to the Latin American financial structure, particularly since several of its main banks were sanctioned following the annexation of Crimea. The most active are the sanctioned bank Vneshekonombank (VBE), which on July of 2013, signed a memorandum of understanding with the Central American Bank of Economic Integration (CABEI).[20] The details of this document have not been released. In December 2014, Russian Gazprombank, also sanctioned, and Argentine Banco de la Nación signed an agreement on cooperation but the details were not made public.[21] Perhaps the most direct inroad to the Latin American financial market is through Evrofinance Monsarbank, a large Russian bank whose largest shareholder is a Venezuelan state-owned National Development Fund (*Fondo Nacional de Desarrollo Nacional*-FONDEN), known for its total lack of transparency in its handling of billions of dollars from the national oil company, PDVSA. FONDEN holds 49.9 percent of the shares of Evrofinance, the other major shareholders include sanctioned banks VBE and Gazprombank.[22]

➢ A Counter-narrative and World View: The Russians have continually used their growing presence to present themselves as a viable alternative to U.S. imperialism in Latin America, a narrative that still has some appeal among the former armed Marxist movements in the region as well as the radical populist movements of the governments and groups affiliated with the ALBA bloc. A constant in the narrative is that a U.S. invasion is imminent and unavoidable. This is because the alleged United States policy is based on pillaging the region's natural resources, toppling the revolutionary regimes leading the march to Latin American independence, and subjugating its citizens. Russia presents itself as an ally against this impending bloodbath, offering to guarantee the security of the new Nicaraguan Canal (if it is ever built), and in return acquiring easier access to deep-water ports in Nicaragua and possibly airfields. Russia has been particularly successful in leveraging this narrative of the anti-imperialist to join multiple Latin American organizations where the U.S. is not welcome. For example, Russia is invited to the meetings of the Community of Latin American and Caribbean States (*Communidad de Estados Latinamericanos y Caribeños* – CELAC), a body set up by Chávez to replace the Organization of American States, from which the United States and Canada are excluded.[23] On March 26, 2015 Russian Foreign Minister Lavrov presented an official solicitation for Russia to become an observer of the Central American

---

[20] http://www.veb.ru/press/news/arch_news/index.php?id_19=30426

[21] Consejo Empresario Argentino-Ruso: "Presentación del banco 'Gazprom' y de empresas rusas productoras de equipos energéticos, de extracción minera y de hidrocarburos en bolsa de comercio en Argentina, accessed at:
http://www.cear.org/index.php?option=com_content&view=article&id=193%3Apresentacion-del-banco-gazprombank-y-de-empresas-rusas-productoras-de-equipos-energeticos-de-extraccion-minera-y-de-hidrocarburos-en-la-bolsa-de-comercio-de-buenos-aires&catid=34%3Anovedades&lang=ru

[22] Daniel Cancel and Corina Rodriguez Pons, "Chavez's Russia Bank Beats Citigroup in Venezuela Bonds Sales," Bloomberg News Service, November 7, 2011, accessed at:
http://www.bloomberg.com/news/articles/2011-11-07/chavez-s-russian-bank-beats-citigroup-in-venezuela-bond-sales

[23] "Russia, CELAC share common foreign policy principles," TASS Russian News Agency, January 31, 2014, accessed at: http://tass.ru/en/russia/717131

Integration System (*Sistema de la Integración Centroamericana* –SICA), Sistema de Integración Centroameicana (SICA).[24] If approved, Russia would have extra-regional observer status at SICA, recently a bulwark of U.S. regional allies. The Foreign Minister's site noted that the request was welcomed unanimously.[25]

In addition IBI Consultants research has mapped an interesting and opaque network of former senior military and KGB officials operating in Central America, primarily running front groups for the Russian military and intelligence services. Through open source mapping, with the help of a Russian language analyst, IBI Consultants was able to track the direct ties of these individuals to the highest levels of the Russian government. The unusual activities of the leaders of this network, made up of multiple companies and trade associations with interlocking directorships of the same "retired" officials is worth further investigation.

The main person in the NK Sesla[26] network we looked at was Alexander Starovoitov, a former general in the Soviet KGB intelligence service. His expensive experience at the highest levels of the Soviet and then Russian intelligence apparatus would likely indicate he is more than just a commercial liaison with potential Latin American clients. His publicly identified specialties include electronic communications technology and cryptography.

Starovoitov is publicly listed as President of NK SESLA, Director General of Inter EVM, and Director of TSITiS. Inter EVM and TSITiS are two related companies operating extensively in Latin America, both of which are closely tied to the Russian defense ministry and the FSB, the successor intelligence agency to the KGB.[27] These organizations, in turn have direct ties to the Russian military and intelligence establishments.

Starovoitov currently holds the rank of General in the Armies Reserve and is the Director of the Cryptography Academy of the Russian Federation and served on Russia's Security Council from 1998-1999. In 1986, Starovoitov received the rank of Major General in the KGB. In 1991, as the Soviet Union collapsed, he was named Director of the Federal Agency of Government Communications and Information of the Russian Federation (FAPSI), roughly

---

[24] "SICA estudia convertir a Rusia en el décimo sexto observador extrarregional," La Vanguardia (March 26, 2015) accessed at: http://www.lavanguardia.com/politica/20150326/54428490520/sica-estudia-convertir-a-rusia-en-el-decimo-sexto-observador-extrarregional.html

[25] The Ministry of Foreign Affairs of the Russian Federation, "Foreign Minister Sergey Lavrov's remarks and answers to questions at a joint news conference with Foreign Minister of Guatemala Carlos Raul Morales following the Russia-Central American Integration System (SICA) meeting in Guatemala," (March 26, 2015) accessed at:
http://archive.mid.ru//brp_4.nsf/0/A93D25A6BF4076EF43257E16002345C3

[26] The acronym stands for Russian National Committee for the Promotion of Economic Trade with Countries of Latin America." It is a non-commercial partnership of several Russian companies and the Russian Ministry of Foreign Affairs. Formed in 1998 with the approval of the office of the Russian President, today it includes high-ranking representatives from various Latin American departments within the Ministry of Foreign Affairs, Ministry of Economic Development, Chamber of Commerce, Rosnauka (Russian Science), the Institute of Latin American of the Russian Academy of Sciences, and other state structures. In Spanish NK SESLA is known at *El Comité Nacional para la Cooperación Económica con los Países Latinoamericanos* (CN CEPLA), accessed at: http://www.cepla.ru/es/about/

[27] NK SESLA Spanish-language website accessed at:
http://www.cepla.ru/es/events/index.php?ELEMENT_ID=11928&phrase_id=90484

the equivalent of the NSA, a post he held for eight years. FAPSI was dissolved in 2003 and folded into the FSB.

Starovoitov, however, does not seem to have fully retired from government service. As the Director General of Inter EVM, meaning the International Center for Informatics and Electronics, he manages a state sponsored Science and Technology and Information Consortium to "jointly solve the problems of the creation and development of advanced information technology, computer hardware and microelectronics."[28]

The Inter EVM website also displays the company's licenses from the FSB and Russian military on behalf of those institutions "using information constituting state secrets," advanced cryptographic information systems, and "activities in the field of information tools."[29] This clearly links the company directly to the most secretive and powerful parts of the Russian state, rather than a simple purveyor of information technology and computer hardware.

The third organization Starovoitov directs is TsITIS - the Center of Informational Technology Systems of Executive Branch Organs, a secretive government agency specializing in signals intelligence and code breaking. President Putin recently charged the company with building a multi-billion dollar integrated, secure communications network for the Russian military. The network is to help detect and deter cyber attacks.[30]

There are other interesting Russian nodes that would benefit from further examination. Particularly in Central America, primarily Panama and Nicaragua, IBI Consultants also found numerous websites in Russian offering a variety of services that are unusual. For example, sites run by a husband and wife team offering real estate in Panama and Nicaragua for sale to Russians also offers clients the ability to "quickly receive a Panamanian passport," register an anonymous Panamanian corporation or Private Interest Foundation.[31]

A new addition to the pro-Russia bloc in Latin America is Salvador Sánchez Cerén, a former Marxist guerrilla leader who assumed the presidency of El Salvador in June 2014. Many of El Salvador's new government senior officials were trained in the Soviet Union, speak Russian and have publicly promised to align their new administration with Putin. Russia, in return, has opened a large trade office in El Salvador with the promise of upgrading it to a major new embassy in short order.[32] The primary Russian contact in El Salvador is José Luis Merino, better know by his nom d'guerre Ramiro Vásquez, a Soviet trained former Communist Party urban commando. Merino, who has publicly been identified as major weapons supplier to the Colombian FARC guerrillas, controls a business empire worth hundreds of millions of dollars where the origin of the money remains a mystery.

---

[28] This was taken from Inter EVM's website, accessed at: http://www.inevm.ru/index.php

[29] Accessed at: http://www.inevm.ru/index.php

[30] "Russian FSB mulls unified secure communications net," Flash Critic Cyber Threat News, August 21, 2013, accessed at: http://flashcritic.com/russian-fsb-mulls-unified-secure-communications-net/

[31] See for example, the website of Advance Trading SA: http://atsa-panama.com/eng/index.html

[32] Russia has embassies and/or consulates in Argentina, Bolivia, Brazil, Chile, Colombia, Ecuador, Guyana, Mexico, Paraguay, Peru, Uruguay, and Venezuela, Costa Rica, Cuba, Guatemala, Mexico, Nicaragua, and Panama. Accessed at: http://www.russianembassy.net/iservice.nsf/samerica and http://www.russianembassy.net/iservice.nsf/namerica

Russia's rise underscores the significant loss of Washington's ability to shape events in a region close to home and of significant strategic interest. This decline, due to waning policy attention amidst multiple global crises and severe budget constraints, is leaving a diminishing group of friends in the hemisphere. Since 2010, U.S. engagement efforts, both military and diplomatic, have been scaled back dramatically with overall aid decreasing both civilian and security assistance. And regional initiatives have been among the hardest hit by the ongoing budget austerity,[33] which has left a vacuum that is being filled by extra-regional actors and a growing group of political leaders who hope for the collapse of the United States.

 While the U.S. position remains preeminent – due to geographic proximity, cultural ties, and trade ties – it is eroding more quickly than is often understood. Also eroding, as Russia and other extra-regional actors such as China and Iran strengthen the hands of ALBA governments, is the long-standing U.S. goal of establishing functioning democracies under the rule of law with stable economic growth. As the U.S. pulls back, it is simultaneously facing a concerted effort by ALBA governments to erase any trace of U.S. military and U.S. security doctrine, weaken economic and cultural ties, and portray any and all U.S. policy decisions as seeking to recolonize Latin America.[34]

This new reality highlights General Kelly's assessment that the United States must remain engaged in the region, and in a much more visible way. In my regular travels to the region there is a strong perception, not always based on reality, that the United States has few policy concerns and little interest in Latin America.

This contrasts sharply with the constant presence of high-level Russian officials from the political, military and intelligence communities that pass through the region and receive overwhelming favorable reviews in the state-controlled media. There is no question in my mind that the State Department, SOUTHCOM and the intelligence community all remain significantly under resourced in Latin America, where resources have been cut and the ability of embassies to carry out some of their core functions has been reduced as has the ability to monitor and understand the Russian activities.

In a time of resource scarcity, Russia has managed to leverage a small amount of resources into significant gains. The Russia agenda is aided and abetted by the ALBA bloc of nations, in

---

[33] From FY 2008 to FY 2012, U.S. aid to Latin America dropped from $2.1 billion to $1.8 billion, a 13 percent drop. See: Peter J. Meyer and Mark P. Sullivan, "U.S. Foreign Assistance to Latin America and the Caribbean: Recent Trends and FY2013 Appropriations, Congressional Research Service, June 26, 2012. In 2013 and 2014, U.S. aid dropped by another 9 percent and 13 percent respectively. See: Adam Isacson et al, 'Time to Listen: Trends in U.S. Security Assistance to Latin America and the Caribbean, 2013, accessed at: http://lawg.org/storage/documents/Time to Listen-Trends in U.S. Security Assistance to Latin America and the Caribbean.pdf. Within this context, funding for USSOUTHCOM has dropped 26 percent in fiscal 2013, after already suffering substantial cuts in previous years. See: "SOUTHCOM's Counter-Drug Efforts Hit by Budget Cuts," Institute for Defense and Government Advancement, April 26, 2014, accessed at: http://www.idga.org/homeland-security/articles/southcom-s-counter-drug-efforts-hit-by-budget-cuts/Adam Isacson et al, 'Time to Listen: Trends in U.S. Security Assistance to Latin America and the Caribbean, 2013, accessed at: http://lawg.org/storage/documents/Time to Listen-Trends in U.S. Security Assistance to Latin America and the Caribbean.pdf.

[34] Farah, op. cit.

which there is little independent media and where the official media magnifies each statement and donation. The United States needs a more visible return to the region to counter the perception and the reality that Russia is again a major strategic influence in the region.

———————

Mr. DUNCAN. Thank you. Before I recognize Dr. Rouvinski, I want to thank you and Dr. Urcuyo for traveling from Costa Rica and Colombia. You all have traveled quite a distance and we are glad we are able to make this hearing happen today. So thank you for that and on behalf of the committee. And Dr. Rouvinski, you are recognized for 5 minutes.

STATEMENT OF VLADIMIR ROUVINSKI, PH.D., DIRECTOR OF THE CIES INTERDISCIPLINARY RESEARCH CENTER, UNIVERSIDAD ICESI IN COLOMBIA

Mr. ROUVINSKI. Thank you very much, Mr. Chairman, Mr. Ranking Member, and the other esteemed committee members, for the opportunity to speak today before the committee. Let me begin my testimony by sharing some general observations with regard to the Russian presence in Latin America, placing a particular emphasis on the evolution of Russian goals and objectives in the Western Hemisphere from the beginning of the 1990s until now.

Following the collapse of the Soviet Union, the political and military, economic and cultural contacts between Russia and Latin America declined sharply. But during the first decade of the 21st century, the situation changed dramatically. Already by 2008, Russian trade with Latin America had doubled in comparison with 1996. The same year, in a new vector, Russia declared its foreign policy to be a strategic partnership with Latin America. By 2015, Russia is maintaining diplomatic relations with all countries in the Western Hemisphere.

With many of these countries the Russian Government signed a visa-free agreement allowing greater ease of travel between the regions. Taking into consideration the dynamic relations between Russia and Latin America, the political leaders in Russia began to talk about the Russian return to Latin America, referring to similarities between the current state of affairs and the policy promoted by the Soviet Union during the Cold War. However, characterizing the Russian presence in the Western Hemisphere as a ''return'' is inaccurate, since the Russian objectives only partially match those pursued by the Soviet Union.

The current Russian strategy in the Western Hemisphere is to strengthen diplomatic relations with all Latin American countries while promoting economic cooperation and the arms trade, as well as military contact with some of the countries.

Three groups of countries in the region can be distinguished in light of these efforts. The first group consists of Venezuela, Nicaragua, and Cuba, which have offered full support to Russia in the Ukrainian and Syrian crises. These countries benefit from Russian cooperation in the energy sector, have been recipient of Russian aid and are major buyer of Russian arms. Their political contacts with Moscow pave the way for military cooperation, thus explicitly challenging the United States in its ''near abroad.'' Russia also seems to expand the area of cooperation with this group by offering collaboration in sensitive issues such as drug trafficking and international organized crime.

The second group includes Argentina, Mexico, and Brazil, the most economically important countries for the region, as well as several other Latin American nations. While the leaders of these countries may not fully collaborate with the Kremlin's international agenda, Russia still counts on their support in various multilateral arrangements including the United Nations, BRICS, and G–20.

The third group of countries has strong ties with the United States and are unwilling to risk their relations with the West, but do not want to antagonize Russia either. An example is Colombia, which is maintaining its alliance with the United States while avoiding confrontation with Russia.

The current Russian economic presence in the Western Hemisphere is very significant if comparing to the state of Russian commerce and trade with the region in the 1990s. However, the Russian economic engagement with Latin America is rather modest in comparison of some other extra-hemispheric actors, firstly, the People's Republic of China. Moreover, it is important to underline that Russia's capacity to further build up its presence in the Western Hemisphere is limited because of the low price of petroleum on international markets and the effect of economic sanctions imposed on the country by the United States and Europe.

While the relations between Russian leaders and many of their Latin American counterparts can be characterized as strongly sympathetic, some of them lack a long-term commitment and may crumble under new leaders. In addition, in the challenging global geopolitical context, Russia has managed to maintain stable relation with all Latin American countries and therefore effectively undermined the efforts of the United States and its allies to isolate Moscow in order to pressure the government of Vladimir Putin to change its current policy in Europe.

I would like to invite the United States House of Representatives to consider the following: The Russian re-engagement with Latin America is evidence that the processes that are taking place in Latin America and the Caribbean are part of the changing global geopolitical landscape, and the answers to the challenges posed to the United States economic and security interests as a result of the Russian return to the region are to be considered from a global perspective.

It is also important to open possibilities for a more comprehensive study of the Russian presence in Latin America by academic institutions and think-tanks in the United States. Whereas in recent years, research activities concerned, for example, with China's presence in the region have been booming, the Russian presence in Latin America has been mostly neglected. However, to better understand the Russian long-term interest in this part of the world, support for academic research is pivotal. Thank you for your time, and I look forward to the questions.

[The prepared statement of Mr. Rouvinski follows:]

HEARING BEFORE THE
HOUSE COMMITTEE ON FOREIGN AFFAIRS

Russian Engagement in the Western Hemisphere

October 22, 2015

Vladimir Rouvinski, Ph.D.
Director, CIES Interdisciplinary Research Center
Icesi University in Colombia

I would like to thank the Chairman Royce, Ranking Member Engel, and the other esteemed committee members for the opportunity to speak before the Committee today.

Originally from Russia, I have moved to Latin America about 20 years ago, and currently I am Director of CIES Research Center at Icesi University located in the city of Cali in Colombia. My primary research interests focus on relations between Russia and Latin America, and, in recent years, I have had an opportunity to travel extensively in the region to conduct field research as well as to coordinate a number of research activities on the topic, in collaboration with researchers in Latin America, Russia, Europe, and the United States. This group organized several academic meetings to present their findings to other researchers, public officials and experts, including the meetings of Latin American Studies Association in Washington, DC in 2013, and in San Juan, Puerto Rico earlier this year.

(1) Overview: the Russian "return" to Latin America

I would like to begin my testimony by sharing some general observations with regard to the Russian presence in Latin America, placing a particular emphasis on the evolution of Russian goals and objectives in the Western Hemisphere from the beginning of the 1990s until now.

Following the collapse of the Soviet Union, the government of Boris Yeltsin seemed to lose all interest in Latin America. During the first part of the 1990s, the political, military, economic, and cultural contacts between Russia and this part of the world declined sharply. This change was particularly noticeable in Cuba, the most important ally that Moscow had in the Western Hemisphere during the Cold War; the commercial turnover between the two countries declined by 69 percent, and, in 2001, Russia closed down the Lourdes Electronic Radar Station which had been used to spy on the United States. In other Latin American nations, the picture was similar. Along with the decline in commerce, political contacts between Russia and the region were reduced to a low level.

But during the first decade of the 21st century, the situation changed dramatically: between 2000 and 2014, Russian presidents travelled seven times to Latin America, and the Russian minister of foreign affairs visited the subcontinent a dozen times.

By 2008, Russian trade with Latin America had doubled from 1996. The same year, in a new vector, Russia declared its foreign policy to be a strategic partnership with Latin America. It aimed at broadening "the political and economic cooperation with . . . Latin American and Caribbean countries and their associations, relying on the progress achieved in relations with the states of this region in recent years," and enhancing "its interaction with these states within international arrangements ," promoting "export of Russia's high-technology products to Latin American countries," and implementing "joint energy, infrastructure and high-tech projects, inter alia, in accordance with the plans developed by the regional integration associations." Important private and state-owned Russian companies, chiefly from the energy sector, took advantage of the favorable political environment and established or strengthened their presence in Latin America.

By 2015, Russia is maintaining diplomatic relations with all countries in the Western Hemisphere. With many of these countries, the Russian government signed a visa-free agreement allowing greater ease of travel between the regions. Additional evidence of the Russian advance into this territory includes the remarkable growth of Russian arms sales to Latin American countries as well as the visits by Russian navy ships and strategic bombers to Venezuela, Nicaragua, and Cuba. Several Latin American leaders openly supported Moscow's stand on conflicts in Georgia and Ukraine.

Taking into consideration the dynamic relations between Russia and Latin America, the political leaders in Russia began to talk about the Russian "return" to Latin America, referring to similarities between the current state of affairs and the policy promoted by the Soviet Union during the Cold War. However, characterizing the Russian presence in the Western Hemisphere as a "return" is inaccurate, since the Russian objectives only partially match those pursued by the Soviet Union. It is also important to recognize that the Russian strategy toward the subcontinent has evolved in line with the changing geopolitical strategy of Moscow.

The beginning of the Russian re-engagement with Latin America in the 1990s can be explained primarily by the interests of the Russian companies in conquering new markets and taking advantage of new opportunities. The famous visit of Yevgeni Primakov to Latin America in 1997 was intended to provide political support in the region for Russian businesses in the energy and military industrial sectors. At the same time, other trade between Russia and the region was growing fast, with Argentina and Brazil at the top of the list of Russian trade partners in Latin America. Meanwhile, a part of Latin America took a political left turn; countries like Brazil, Venezuela, Nicaragua, Ecuador, Argentina, and Bolivia were now ruled by leftist or populist leaders. At that point, Russian leaders were careful not to align themselves publicly with the anti-American rhetoric of the Latin American leftist presidents, but this has changed because of the shifting of Russian global strategy following the war with Georgia in August, 2008. Moscow regarded the diplomatic recognition by Nicaragua and Venezuela of the breakaway Georgian republics of Abkhazia and South Ossetia as evidence of international support for the Russian stand in the conflict, and that Russia was capable of operating in the US "near abroad". Hence, the arrival of Russian navy ships and strategic bombers at Venezuela was a message clearly directed to the United States after it sent its navy ships to the Black Sea. From this perspective, the 2014-

2015 Russian response to the Ukrainian crisis in Latin America was similar to that of 2008. Whereas only a few of Latin American countries openly supported the Russian annexation of the Crimean peninsula, Moscow maintained stable relations with every Latin American nation and mitigated the efforts of the United States and its allies to isolate Russia. However, the economic ties between Russia and several Latin American nations have not been as enduring. Many Russian companies from the energy sector eventually left the region, and the arms trade has suffered major setbacks in recent years.

(2) The Russian strategy in the Western Hemisphere

The current Russian strategy in the Western Hemisphere is to strengthen diplomatic relations with Latin American countries while promoting economic cooperation and the arms trade. Russia

Three groups of countries in the region can be distinguished in light of these efforts. The first group consists of Venezuela, Nicaragua, and Cuba, which have offered full support to Russia in the Ukrainian and Syrian crises. These countries benefit from Russian cooperation in the energy sector, have been recipients of Russian aid and are major buyers of Russian arms. They are also willing to let Russian air and naval forces use their territory.

The second group includes Argentina, Mexico, and Brazil, the most economically important countries of the region, as well as several other Latin American nations. While the leaders of these countries may not fully collaborate with the Kremlin's international agenda, Russia still counts on their support in various multilateral arrangements, including the United Nations, BRICS, and G-20.

The third group of countries has strong ties with the United States and are unwilling to risk their relations with the West in order to please Moscow, but do not want to antagonize Russia, either. An example is Colombia, which is maintaining its alliance with the United States while avoiding confrontation with Russia.

Let me illustrate the above observations by taking a closer look at some of the bilateral relations between Russian and countries of Latin America.

(3) Russia and Venezuela

For today's Russian general public, Venezuela is the most recognizable country in Latin America. This is because of the high number of visits of the Venezuelan leaders to Russia and extensive coverage of the country's relations with Moscow by the Russian mass media. The evolution of Russian relations with Venezuela clearly demonstrates the shift in Russian strategies in Latin America.

In Venezuela, amongst the powerful Russian privately and state-owned corporations that were gaining access to this South-American market in the 2000s, one could find many of the most important Russian companies, including Gazprom, Rosneft, Lukoil, Surgutneftegaz, and TNK-BP. In 2010, a major contract was agreed upon between the Russian National Petroleum Consortium (NNK12) and Petroleos de Venezuela SA (PdVSA), concerning the start of a joint venture to explore the Venezuelan oil reserves in the Orinoco River area. It was expected that the total investments in this project would reach between 20 and 30 billion dollars during the next twenty-five years.

Any discussion of Russian-Venezuelan relations during the period in question would be incomplete without mentioning the arms trade between the two countries. Since 2005, Russia has supplied Venezuela with a hundred thousand Kalashnikov automatic rifles, twenty-four Su-30MK2 fighter jets and approximately fifty helicopters, at a total cost estimated at 4 billion dollars. This constituted a dramatic breakthrough by Russia into the Latin American arms market, and it also caused alarm bells to ring for traditional arms sellers in the region as well as by some of Venezuela's neighboring countries.

However, today there are evidences that the official discourse, which emphasizes the equally attractive benefits of the Russian trade and energy collaboration with Venezuela, is far from telling the whole story. It seems that, in reality, some of the Russian companies, with already established presence in Venezuela, fear any further involvement and even try to leave the country because of the political instability and variety of other business risks.

By contrast to the situation with energy cooperation and trade, the political contacts between Moscow and Caracas during the recent years had strengthened transforming Venezuela, along with Nicaragua and Cuba, into a major Russian key ally in the Western Hemisphere. This collaboration included the support by the government of Venezuela of the Russian stand in the Georgian 2008 war and the conflict in Ukraine as well as an offer to station Russian air and naval forces in the country. The current President of Venezuela Nicolas Maduro managed to maintain country's close political ties with the Russian leaders as Hugo Chavez did in the past.

(4) Russia and Nicaragua

In 2008, Russian foreign strategy changed dramatically as a result of the first war between Russia and one of the former Soviet republics. When Moscow ordered its troops to cross the border with Georgia, the Kremlin was expecting the West not to intervene, since the South Caucasus was considered by Russia as part of its "near abroad." However, the reaction of the Western powers was a strong one, and, above all, it was the coverage of the war by the Western mass media that turned the Russian military victory into its international public opinion defeat. Hence, the announcement of the decision by the government of Nicaragua to recognize both of the separatist republics as new independent states on September 5, 2008 was extremely timely. Russia rushed to show its appreciation of the Central American nation: in December 2008, Moscow opened a credit line to Nicaragua and an agreement with the Russian state-owned company Inter RAO EES to build several small- and medium-sized hydroelectric and geothermal plants in Nicaragua was signed. A close cooperation between two countries continued ever after. The plans of opening of a counternarcotic training facility had been announced, and the high-ranking Russian military officials became frequent visitors to this Central American nation. Today, Nicaragua continues to fully support Russia at the international stage.

(5) Russia and Colombia

Colombia was one of the first Latin American countries to establish diplomatic relations with the Soviet Union back in 1935. An Embassy and a Cultural Center were opened in 1943, and were used to spread Marxist ideology in the region. However, following the assassination of a very popular political leader Jorge Eliécer Gaitán, the diplomatic relations were broken and not restored till almost two decades later. In general terms, the interactions between Moscow and Bogota during this time remained limited to energy sector and university training of Colombian students in the Soviet Union. It is worth of mentioning here that several of the top FARC leaders were educated in the Soviet Union and speak fluent Russian.

In the mid-1990s, Moscow was one of only a few countries that openly supported the President Ernesto Samper after he was accused of receiving money from the Cali drug cartel, and then the Russian Minister of Foreign Affairs Yevgenii Primakov was the only high-ranking diplomat from outside Latin America who visited Bogota back then. In return, Russia was given a contract to supply a number of transport helicopters for the Colombian army, and, about the same time, a couple of Russian oil companies obtained licenses for oil exploration in Colombia.

However, after the end of Samper's term, Russia's political, economic and cultural contacts with Colombia had been rather insignificant. It was, on the one hand, the worsening of relations between Colombia and Venezuela, and, on the other hand, the beginning of Moscow's rapprochement with Venezuela that triggered an alarm in Bogota. After an arms deal was made between Russia and Venezuela, the Minister Lavrov had to visit Bogota in order to give assurances to the President Alvaro Uribe Velez that the deal is not meant to jeopardize Colombian security. Another episode that two countries had to find the way to deal with was the incident with the Russian strategic bombers entering the Colombian airspace without a permission of the Colombian authorities. Since the planes were flying from Nicaragua to Venezuela at the very moment when the tensions were high because of a territorial dispute of Nicaragua with Colombia in the Caribbean, the violation of the Colombian airspace was perceived by in the country as a sign of Moscow's support of Nicaragua.

Despite of the above-mentioned episodes, Russia is trying not to jeopardize its relations with Bogota. Colombia is important for Moscow because it offers an opportunity to demonstrate that attempts at international isolation of Russia following the crisis in Ukraine were not successful. Earlier this year, the Russian Embassy in Bogota was able to organize a celebration of the 80th anniversary of the establishment of diplomatic relations between two countries, and the Colombian President Juan Manuel Santos, as well as the Minister of Foreign Affairs Maria Angela Holguin met the Russian Minister of Foreign Affairs Lavrov, who visited the Colombian capital on this occasion.

(6) Impact on the Region and the Implications for the United States

The current Russian economic presence in the Western Hemisphere is very significant if compared to the state of Russian commerce and trade with the region in the 1990s. In some cases, it is now about the Russian incidence in the countries and areas, where Moscow did not have any noteworthy footsteps before, in particular, with regard to arms sales. However, the Russian economic engagement with Latin America is rather modest in comparison with that of some other extra-hemispheric actors, firstly, the People's Republic of China. Moreover, it is important to underline that Russia's capacity to further build up its presence in the Western Hemisphere is limited because of the low price of petroleum on international markets and the effect of economic sanctions imposed on the country by the United States and Europe. While the relations between Russian leaders and many of their Latin American counterparts can be characterized as strongly sympathetic, some of them lack a long-term commitment and may crumble under new leaders.

At the same time, political contacts between Russia and a number of Latin American nations, in particular, Venezuela, Cuba, and Nicaragua have intensified and paved the way for military cooperation with these countries thus explicitly challenging the United States in its "near abroad". Russia also seems to expand the areas of cooperation by offering collaboration in sensitive issues such as drug trafficking and international organized crime in the countries, where in recent years the capacity of the United States to cope with the issues have been reduced. In addition, in the challenging global geopolitical context, Russia has managed to maintain stable relations with all Latin American countries and therefore effectively undermined the efforts of the United States and its allies to isolate Moscow in order to pressure the government of Vladimir Putin to change its current policy in Europe.

(7) Recommendations

I would like to invite the United States House of Representatives to consider the following:

The Russian re-engagement with Latin America is evidence that the processes that are taking place in Latin America and the Caribbean are part of the changing global geopolitical landscape, and the answers to the challenges posed to the United States economic and security interests as a result of the Russian return to the region are to be considered from a global perspective.

It is also important to open possibilities for a more comprehensive study of the Russian presence in Latin America by academic institutions and think-tanks in the United States. Whereas in recent years, research activities concerned with China's presence in the region have been booming, the Russian presence in Latin America has been mostly neglected. However, to better understand the Russian long-term interests in this part of the world, support for academic research is pivotal.

Mr. DUNCAN. Thank you so much for your testimony.

Dr. Urcuyo, is that microphone on?

Mr. URCUYO. Yes.

Mr. DUNCAN. Okay. Make sure it is pointed right at your mouth too. That will be good.

STATEMENT OF CONSTANTINO URCUYO, PH.D., ACADEMIC DIRECTOR, CENTRO DE INVESTIGACIÓN Y ADIESTRAMIENTO POLÍTICO ADMINISTRATIVO IN COSTA RICA

Mr. URCUYO. Okay. Thank you for the invitation. Russia has been present in the region in a new way since the last decade, although Moscow did have great activity during the Cold War. This inheritance will play a role in the current phase because thousands of Latin Americans were trained in the USSR. What is happening in what the Russians call their "near abroad" is interacting in real time with events in Latin America. Russia's diplomatic and military penetration in Latin America is a response to what it sees as an excessive presence of the U.S.A. and NATO in what it considers its influence area.

Besides, Russia is nostalgic for having lost the Soviet empire and wants to show the world that it still a member of the major powers and capable of projecting power in its main adversary's backyard. On the other hand, Putin plays to his domestic audience. The resurgence of great Russian nationalism is fostered by the audacity of its leader. From the perspective of Russian Grand Strategy, forays into the region may not provide significant immediate returns in terms of the global scenario, but in the event of a more generalized future conflict they could enable Russia to use regional internal conflicts to its advantage.

I will focus on Nicaragua due to Russia's importance to this country as well as the potential consequences of its activity for Costa Rica and the rest of Central America. Russia has a historical background of close relations with Managua. Currently, though, collaboration links have become closer. The Russian ministers of defense and foreign affairs visit frequently and a Russian anti-drug training center has opened near Managua.

Russia has also shown interest in deploying satellite stations in Nicaragua for their global positioning system. Russia's focus on anti-drug cooperation is paradoxical if one considers that the drug-dealing routes that go through Nicaragua are not headed to Moscow. Some observers interpret it as a form of covert and strategic expansion. Russia's intention could be to obtain military bases or to trade political military assets as it did during the Cuban missile crisis.

On the other hand, Nicaragua's ongoing maritime conflict with Colombia suggests that its rearmament is aimed more at the confrontation with this country than the fight against organized crime. Such remilitarization has raised concerns. There is great unease about its consequences for the regional balance of forces.

The link between Russia and Nicaragua goes beyond military issues. It involves the diplomatic arena. Since 2008, Nicaragua recognized Abkhazia and South Ossetia in alignment with Russian diplomacy. The alignment was repeated when Nicaragua voted against the disapproval Crimea's annexation at the United Nations. The Russian military and diplomatic presence in Central America is a factor of regional instability. It is threatening for Costa Rica because the country does not have an army and has a border dispute with Nicaragua. If a conflict arises with Colombia, Bogota's level of armament and military training will escalate its dimensions, threatening peace throughout the Caribbean Basin.

Conclusions and recommendations. Russia is trying to transfer its conflict with the U.S. to Latin America while profiting from weapons sales and challenging and provoking the U.S. Latin American countries must be aware that they cannot be trapped in a Russian conflict. Russia's regional old friends and new allies provide a haven for extra-hemispheric powers that seek to counterbalance the power of the U.S.A. by strengthening anti-imperialist nationalism.

Russia's overtures revolve around the military and not around human development. That Russian activity raises apprehension in Washington is understandable. However, the answer cannot be unilateral. It must emerge from a dialogue with Latin American countries that considers all national interests and defines multilateral political partnerships.

China's active economic cooperation frees some of Moscow's Latin American allies from economic pressures enabling Russian military and diplomatic penetration. The recent Chinese-Russian partnership could develop in the future through greater coordination in the hemisphere. There are speculations about the likely participation of Russia in the defense of the Nicaraguan Canal by the Chinese.

Russian actions in Central America demand a more detailed accounting of its intense military cooperation with Nicaragua. Russia actually is trying to play a new role in Central America becoming an observer member of the Central American Integration System. Some Latin American countries have given a positive response to Vladimir Putin's initiatives, which shows that inter-American relations have shifted qualitatively. It is important, last, to develop a shared and strategic doctrine in the Americas adapted to the new architecture of the international system. Thank you.

[The prepared statement of Mr. Urcuyo follows:]

<u>OPENING STATEMENT BY DR. CONSTANTINO URCUYO-FOURNIER</u>

<u>BEFORE THE</u> <u>UNITED STATES HOUSE SUBCOMMITTEE ON THE WESTERN HEMISPHERE</u>

<u>AT A HEARING CONVENED TO DISCUSS</u>

<u>RUSSIA'S ENGAGEMENT IN THE WESTERN HEMISPHERE</u>

OCTOBER 22, 2015

Mr Chairman, Ranking Member Sires:

Thanks for the invitation to address the subcommittee on a matter of utmost importance both for the USA and Latin America.

The international order is undergoing a deep and accelerated change process that affects the major powers as well as medium and small-sized countries.
Latin America is engaged in this process and is affected both by external issues and internal transformations.

1- The engagement of extra-hemispheric actors (China, Iran, Russia) has become stronger and the shift to the left in several countries (Venezuela, Nicaragua, Ecuador, Bolivia) transforms Inter-American power relations..

2- Brazil's participation in the BRICS group and the G20 places the region in the dynamics of the emerging powers..

3- The trends towards a multipolar world has granted more autonomy to the external policies of many of the countries of the region.

4- There is a trend towards the shaping of sub-regional blocks, defined by political-ideological alignment. The Alliance of the Pacific (Colombia, México,

Peru and México) should be added to this panorama, this group is center-focused and interested in the TPP.

5- Also, there are geopolitical differences between the countries in the North and the South of the region. The first keep more intense relations with the USA than the second.

6- Russia has been present in the region in a new way since the last decade, although Moscow did have great activity during the Cold War supporting the Cuban regime and revolutionary guerrillas. This inheritance from the past will play a role in the current phase, because thousands of Latin Americans were trained in Russia and in countries like Cuba and Nicaragua. There are groups that speak Russian and are familiar with the Russian culture.

The Russian comeback is different from the Chinese presence. The Chinese have more involvement in the economic area even if they have long-term strategic interests. The Russians are more involved in military exchanges and security matters, especially since the falling prices of hydrocarbons and economic sanctions have hindered their economic revival.

Moscow's foray into the USA's traditional space is a challenge to US foreign policy. Why is Russia set on establishing these links and connections, marked by constant visits by its Ministers of Foreign Affairs and Defense, and capped by Putin's own presence in 2014.

These policies are linked to changes in the international order. Consider Dr. Henry Kissinger's statement in an appearance before the Armed Services Committee early this year:

1- The international order is being globally redefined;

2- The concept of order inside each region is being challenged or redefined;

3- Relations amongst world regions are being redefined;

4- "...for the first time in history, every region now interacts in real time and affects each other simultaneously."

This last aspect is key to explaining Russia's new presence. What is happening in what the Russians call their "near abroad" is interacting in real time with events in Latin America. Russia's diplomatic and military penetration is a response to what it sees as an excessive presence of the USA and NATO in what they consider their influence area.

Besides, Russia is nostalgic for having lost the Soviet Empire and wants to show the world that it is still a member of the major powers and capable of projecting power in its main adversary's backyard.

On the other hand, Putin plays to his domestic audience. The resurgence of great Russian nationalism is fostered by the audacity of a leader that enters the influence area of the United States of America.

From the perspective of Russian Grand Strategy, forays into the region may not provide significant immediate returns in terms of the global scenario, but in the event of a more generalized future conflict, they could enable Russia to use regional internal conflicts to its advantage, thus becoming a major distraction factor for US strategy.

The specific manifestations of the Russian presence have been diverse and vary from country to country.

The Russian connection with the region happens through old allies of the USSR; through countries willing to counteract US influence; or through neutral allies over which Russia has some strategic interest.[1]

---

[1] R Evan Ellis. Russian Engagement in Latin America and the Caribbean: Return to the "Strategic Game" in a Complex- Interdependent Post-Cold War World?. Strategic Studies Institute. US Army War College. Carlisle. April 2015.

Russian activity is relevant in Cuba, Venezuela and Nicaragua, countries with which it keeps important links. It is also important in Ecuador, Bolivia, Argentina and Brazil, but today we need not elaborate on its presence in these countries. It is enough to say that it is focused on security issues—Russia lacks the economic resources and wherewithal to enter into meaningful economic cooperation or trade relations with these countries.

This reality elevates the profile of military cooperation with Nicaragua and Venezuela, which takes the form of weapons sales and the intent to establish a permanent military presence in both countries.

I will focus my presentation on Nicaragua, due to Russia's importance to this country as well as the potential consequences of its activity for Costa Rica and the rest of Central America.

Nicaragua: Russia's gateway to Central America.

Russia has a historical background of close relations with Managua in terms of political, military and educational terms. Currently, though, collaboration links have become closer. The Russian ministers of Defense and Foreign Affairs visit frequently and a Russian antidrug training center has opened near Managua.

The reach of that training center is not limited to Nicaragua. Police forces from El Salvador and Guatemala have already been trained there by Russians. It is important to highlight the training received by Salvadorians, given the historic ties of their governing party, the FMLN, with the USSR during the guerrilla years.

Russia has also shown interest in deploying satellite stations in Nicaragua for their global positioning system (GLONASS).[2]

Russia's focus on antidrug cooperation is paradoxical if one considers that the drug-dealing routes that go through Nicaragua are not headed to Moscow. Some observers interpret it as a form of covert, strategic expansion. Russia's intention could be to obtain military bases as regional beachheads or to trade political military assets as it did during the Cuban missile crisis

The announcement of a potential sale of Russian frigates and of Mig-29s to Nicaragua, supposedly to combat drug trafficking, also raises suspicions. Such bellicose materiel is not precisely the best tool to fight this type of crime.

On the other hand, Nicaragua's ongoing maritime conflict with Colombia suggests that its rearmament is aimed more at the confrontation with this country than the fight against organized crime.

Such remilitarization has raised concern among countries in the Caribbean Basin. There is great unease about its consequences for the regional balance of forces, particularly as it will break the security treaties signed in the 80's at the end of the Central American wars.

The president of Costa Rica, Luis Guillermo Solís stated[3] during a trip to Europe:

"We are very concerned about the continuous presence of high authorities of the Russian government in Nicaragua such as the Minister of Defense, and the presence of armed vessels of the Russian Navy in the waters of that country".

---

[2] http://actualidad.rt.com/actualidad/173657-nicaragua-instalacion-estacion-sistema-ruso-glonass

A few months earlier, the Minister of Foreign Affairs, Manuel González, had also expressed his apprehension about the Russian[3] Minister of Foreign Affairs while in Guatemala and to Secretary of State John Kerry[4].

The link between Russia and Nicaragua goes beyond military issues: it involves the diplomatic arena, supported by the anti-American stance of the Sandinistas.[3]

Since 2008, Nicaragua recognized Abkhazia and South Ossetia in alignment with Russian diplomacy. The alignment was repeated when voting against the disapproval of Crimea's annexation at the UN. Managua's position goes along with the Russian Doctrine that postulates the development of a multipolar world to counterbalance the hegemony of the United States.

Diplomacy has gone further in other ways. Russia donated 100,000 yearly tons of flour to Nicaragua between 2011 and 2014 as well as 500 cars to be used as taxis, 520 public-service buses and 41 million dollars for a new hospital in Managua.[4]

Recapitulating, the Russian military and diplomatic presence in Central America is a factor of regional instability because it disrupts the balance of forces. It is threatening for Costa Rica because the country does not have an army and has a border dispute with Nicaragua. If a conflict arises with Colombia, Bogota's level of armament and military training will escalate its dimensions, threatening peace throughout the Caribbean Basin.

Conclusions and Recommendations.

1- Russia is trying to transfer its conflict with the USA to other regions of Latin America while profiting from weapons sales and challenging and provoking the USA.

---

[3] http://actualidad.rt.com/actualidad/166283-nicaragua-apoyar-iniciativas-putin-ucrania
[4] Confidencial, Managua 12/2/2015

2- Latin American countries must be aware that they cannot be trapped in a Russian conflict.

3- Russia's regional old friends and new allies provide a haven for extra-hemispheric powers that seek to counterbalance the power of the USA, by strengthening anti-imperialist nationalism against Washington.

4- Russia's overtures revolve around the military and not around human development.

5- That Russian activity raises apprehension on the banks of the Potomac is understandable. However, the answer cannot be unilateral. It must emerge from a dialogue with Latin American countries that considers all national interests and defines multilateral political partnerships around mutual prosperity and human development.

6- China's active economic cooperation frees some of Moscow's Latin American allies from economic pressures, enabling Russian military and diplomatic penetration in the Western Hemisphere. Part of the conversations between USA and Peking should focus on raising awareness that, even though their involvement in Latin America is not in the area of security, it can have consequences for security.

7- The recent Chinese-Russian partnership could develop in the future through greater coordination of their policies in the hemisphere. There are speculations about the likely participation of Russia in the defense of the Nicaraguan Canal promoted by Chinese corporations.

8- Russian actions in Central America demand a more detailed accounting of its intense military cooperation with Nicaragua. Nicaragua's rearmament, fostered by Russia, disrupts the balance of regional forces, achieved at a high cost after the end of the civil wars of the nineteen-eighties.

9- Some Latin American countries have given a positive response to Vladimir Putin's initiatives, which shows that Inter-American relations have shifted qualitatively. This demands the exploration of new cooperation paths with the US to ensure shared security in a context quite unlike that of the Cold War.

10- It is important to develop a shared strategic thought in the Americas, adapted to the new architecture of the international system. In it, all conflict scenarios interact in real time. It is no longer valid to act in an isolated manner, without taking the global panorama into account.

11- Challenges to Central American security are not restricted to the so-called War against Drugs. Excessive attention to this issue can blind us to the active presence of extra-hemispheric actors who could use regional conflicts to divert attention from their own conflicts in other spots around the globe.

———

Mr. DUNCAN. Thank you so much.

Dr. Negroponte, for 5 minutes.

STATEMENT OF DIANA VILLIERS NEGROPONTE, PH.D., PUBLIC POLICY SCHOLAR, WOODROW WILSON INTERNATIONAL CENTER FOR SCHOLARS

Ms. NEGROPONTE. Thank you, Mr. Chairman and Ranking Member Sires, for the opportunity to present ideas this afternoon. Having listened to my three colleagues I am going to adapt somewhat my remarks this afternoon, but I have left with you a written testimony.

I wish to look at the issue of Russian engagement in a somewhat distinct way and analyze why Russia has become more active in this hemisphere. I would argue there are three reasons. First, Russia needs markets, markets for its military equipment, its heavy industrial goods, and its growing IT sector. It was interesting when President Putin visited Nicaragua last year and it was at the last moment that he asked Nicaragua to sell fruits, vegetables, coffee, and meat given that Russia had banned the import of these important products from its natural and normal sources. Markets, I would argue, is one of the reasons why Russia has expanded its interest and its presence.

Secondly, Russia needs friends. It needs friends at the U.N. General Assembly. It needs friends who will vote with it against the United States when we condemn the annexation of Korea and activities in Ukraine.

The third reason for Russia is as the West has expanded its presence in the Baltics, in Ukraine and Poland, Russia has sought to meddle in what might be called by some "our backyard." The response from both Nicaragua and Cuba has been interesting because of its distinctiveness. In the case of Nicaragua, as Dr. Urcuyo has pointed out, Daniel Ortega is playing high risks. He discusses the purchase of MiG-29s, eight of them, from Russia. He has developed a training center for military helicopters and there are no funds to pay for this.

So there is a lot of rhetoric and hype, but the reality on the ground is that we are bumbling along. What is not bumbling along and what is of interest to the Central Americans is the development of the regional training center for anti-drug cooperation, and that is useful for the Hondurans, Salvadorans and Guatemalans. Were the United States to be more effective and more general in its anti-drug and its anti-narcotics program, those countries would have less reason to look toward Russia.

In the case of Raul Castro, he is more cautious and more calculating than Daniel Ortega. Raul Castro has been blind-sided by the Russians and previously the Soviet Union. You will recall 1962. And in 2008, a similar by Russia to place missile systems in Cuba was found out only later by Raul Castro much to his disapproval and irritation. Therefore, on the part of Raul Castro, there is skepticism and care in dealing with Russia. He is not going to be blindsided again.

What is the recommendation for us in the United States? We should pass the billion-dollar program to support Central America. The underlying problems of the region are poverty and unequal distribution of wealth. If we are not to show that we care about these underlying problems exacerbated further by the drug trade, exacerbated further by the presence of military weapons, then we should expect that others will fill that space. I sincerely hope that space is not filled by Russia. Thank you.

[The prepared statement of Ms. Negroponte follows:]

Russian Engagement in the Western Hemisphere
Testimony before the House Foreign Affairs Committee,
Subcommittee on Western Hemisphere
October 22, 2015
Diana Villiers Negroponte, JD, Ph.D.
Public Policy Scholars, Woodrow Wilson International Center for Scholars

Honorable members of the Subcommittee on Western Hemisphere Affairs, my remarks today will focus on Russian engagement in Cuba and Central America.

In December 1991, the dissolving Soviet Union withdrew its financial support from Cuba and through the island to Nicaragua and the guerilla forces in El Salvador. The result was a victory for democratic governance in Nicaragua and the January 1992 peace agreement in El Salvador. Removal of Soviet and then Russian support for regimes that were opposed to U.S. liberal democracy and free market economies paved the way for 20 years of relative peace in Central America. Today, the return of Russian trade, investment and prospective military projects in the Western Hemisphere is not a return to the proxy fights of the Cold War, but instead indicates Russian outreach in the search for markets and friends. European and U.S. sanctions have driven Russia to look for alternative countries who can buy their hardware, enter into joint ventures on energy products and provide votes in Russia's favor at the UN General Assembly.

In 1992 Russia inherited the close Soviet alliance between Moscow and Havana. But whereas over the previous 33 years the Soviet Union could subsidize the Cuban economy with oil, trucks, tourists and military hardware to the tune of $4-5 billion a year, Russia after 1992 did not have the cash to maintain its economic support to the island. A decade long quieting of Cuban/Russian relations followed with Fidel Castro urging citizens to adapt, find their own resources and make do with very little. The size of the Cuban debt to Russia in January 1992 was estimated by Russians to be $25-26 billion.

Fidel Castro turned to Hugo Chavez of Venezuela to support the island's energy needs through *Petrocaribe*. In exchange, Castro sent doctors and intelligence officers to Venezuela. Fidel recognized that his Soviet supporters were unable to maintain the annual subsidy, but he did not wish to lose a relationship that had given him leverage throughout the hemisphere. Fidel and later Raul Castro maintained the relationship with Moscow, visiting Russia and welcoming Russian visitors. Both considered that Gorbachev was naïve and that *glasnost* (freedoms of the press and expression) would destroy the Soviet system. Both determined, therefore, to maintain control over free speech on the island. Raul has opened up the economy somewhat with his creation of small business opportunities and most recently the normalization of relations with the United States, but the old Soviet system of political control and state intelligence gathering continues. Freedom House, of which I am a trustee, still classifies Cuba as 'Not Free.'

So what is the nature of the Cuban/Russian relationship?

- In December 2000, newly elected President Putin visited Havana. He announced no major agreements or investments, but the visit marked the resumption of high level visits by Cuban-Russian officials. It was also marked by a new degree of pragmatism: then Foreign Minister Igor Ivanov stressed that the relationship would be based upon "the realities" of each country and the competitive rules of the international trading system.[1] Pragmatic trading relations would guide commerce between the two countries and in the ensuing years $166 million of Cuban debt incurred during the Cold War years was restructured.[2]

- Russian restructuring of Cuban debt became a regular fixture until 2014. A percentage of the debt is restructured AND Cuba buys or leases Russian aircraft. The value of the sale or lease agreement often approaches the amount of restructured interest due!

- In 2004, $166 million of Cuban debt to Russia was restructured and two VIP convertible Ilyushin planes were leased for $110 million. In 2006, Russia provided a $325 million export guarantee and *Cubana de Aviación* purchased two Ilyushin and three Tupolev aircraft. Payment of the interest on the loan is due to be completed in 2016.

- In July 2008, Igor Sechin then Deputy-Prime Minister and president of the energy group Rosneft headed a business mission to Cuba and Latin America. Sechin, who speaks good Spanish, noted that trade with Cuba had grown to more than $360 million without specifying whether this amount included the new line of credit. Nevertheless he could point to a 32 percent rise in the number of Russian tourists visiting the island.

- In September 2008, Russia's International Investment Bank (IIB) succeeded in bringing a claim against the Cuban Central Bank for $330 million. IIB could legally seize Cuban assets anywhere in the world, including Cuba, but it chose not to do so. Two months later, then-Russian President Dimitri Medyedev visited Havana to announce the start of new IIB loans to Cuba. Implicit in this announcement was a renegotiation of the outstanding monies owed by Cuba's Central Bank. The Bank has no website and few telephones and according to Russian sources "has been avoiding contact with the IIB for the last several years."[3]

- In February 2013, Prime Minister Medvedev returned to Cuba to restructure Cuba's outstanding debt, which then stood at $32.5 billion. 90 percent of the debt was written off while the remainder would be refinanced over 10 years. (Payment of this debt is complicated because it was acquired in convertible rubles, a currency that no longer exists.) Nevertheless, both governments have sought to resolve the debt issue so that the Cuban government could lease 8 more Russian jets, valued at $650 million.[4]

- In March 2015, Foreign Minister Sergei Lavrov visited Cuba and endorsed Cuban negotiations with the United States. However, no financial or commercial agreements were announced, leaving observers to conclude that Russia was in a wait-and-see mode on the conclusion of Cuba's normalization talks with the United States. Russian pragmatism requires that any further extension of credit, or the payment on existing loans be protected by new Cuban regulations.

- In April 2015, the IIB announced that any extensions of loans would depend upon events within Cuba. Meantime, the Russian firm UVZ-Logistik announced a joint venture with the Cuban metallurgy and engineering firm GESIME to provide machine tools and manufacturing services to support freight

[1] Igor Ivanov, "Rusia y América Latina: Relaciones de cara al futuro," Embassy of the Russian Federation in Chile, January 2001, www.chile.mid.ru/Old/putlag5.html.

[2] "Cuba Profile," Latin American Herald Tribune, www.laht.com/article.asp?ArticleId=393167&CategoryID=13848

[3] "Bank Wins $33 million in Suit v. Cuba," Kommersant September 4, 2008, http://www.kommersant.com/p1020308/Cuban_Soviet_debt

[4] Alexei Anishchuk, "Russia leases planes to Cuba, writes off Soviet debt," Reuters, February 21, 2013, www.reuters.com/article/2013/02/22/us-russia-cuba-deals-idUSBRE91L04J20130222.

wagons, as well as Cuban steel mills and sugar industry at an estimated cost of $25 million.[5] That same month, Russia also agreed to furnish Cuba with two Ansat light helicopters, which should be sold onwards to other Latin American and Caribbean nations.[6] The IIB announced that any extensions of loans would depend upon events within Cuba and meantime Russian financing would be placed on hold. It is clear that Moscow awaits changes to Cuban investment laws that are intended to provide protection to foreign investors.

- Finally, in July this year, President Raul Castro visited Moscow. Once again solidarity and brotherly love was expressed. Particularly, Putin thanked the Cuban leader for opposing UN General Assembly resolutions condemning Russian action in Ukraine.[7] However, beyond the rhetoric and photographs no commercial deals were signed.

Commercial relations have underpinned the renewed bilateral and mutual friendship, but were it not for the sale and lease of high-priced aircraft, the real value in bilateral trade would be meager. Economic, energy and trade ties have replaced the geo-political ties of the Cold War, but financing is problematic with Russian ability to subsidize its Cuban friends severely affected by the falling value of oil and the ruble. It takes two to samba and the Cuban economy remains weak.

Putin had hopes for significant oil and gas development from Cuba's offshore oil fields, but the four Russian contracts to drill beginning in 2010 have not produced the quantity of oil to make the exploration profitable. Difficult geology, problems with the oil rig and the embargo on the use of U.S. made equipment led to termination in 2013. It would appear that Russia welcomes Cuba's resumption of diplomatic and commercial relations with the United States, which should lead to a sound FDI regime.

Russia's Engagement in Central America:

In line with seeking friends and maintaining open lines of communication, Foreign Minister Lavrov and Defense Minister Shoygn have visited Guatemala, El Salvador, Honduras and Nicaragua. President Putin also dropped by in Managua in June 2014 after Daniel Ortega protested that he was visiting Cuba and South America without paying him a call. Putin changed his plans to land in Managua for a few hours after leaving Cuba and endorsed the recently constructed *Centro Regional de Capacitación Antidrogas*. Supported by Russian funds, the center trains security officials from all over Central America.

Development of trade ties is rudimentary between the region and Russia; in 2012 bilateral trade with Nicaragua stood at $110 million and trade with Honduras stood at $51 million. Both Putin and Foreign Minister Lavrov have also encouraged the Nicaraguans to sell them fresh fruits, vegetables, coffee and beef after European imports of these products were banned in Russia.

However, Nicaraguan President, Daniel Ortega's expressed interest in acquiring Mig-29 aircraft with which to fight drug traffickers suggests that he wishes to increase Nicaraguan military power and

---

[5] "Cuban freight wagon joint venture agreement," C & S America, April 27, 2015.
http://www.railwaygazette.com/news/news/cs-america/single-view/view/cuban-freight-wagon-joint-venture-agreement.html
[6] "Cuba-Russia Agree on 5 Year Plan" Havana Times, April 26, 2015, http://www.havanatimes.org/?p=110867
[7] Cuba Defends Russia, Criticizes Economic Sanctions, NATO's Expansion in Eastern Europe," International Business Times, July 16, 2015 "http://www.ibtimes.com/cuba-defends-russia-criticizes-economic-sanctions-natos-expansion-eastern-europe-2011909

influence in the region. Recently, Honduras bought Super Tucano's from Brazil and Colombia bought C-7kfir from Israel, but neither have the firepower of the Mig-29.[8] Valued at $29 million apiece, Nicaraguan citizens are concerned by Ortega's fascination with military prowess rather than social projects in the second poorest country of the Western Hemisphere.

Were the sale of the Mig-29 to go forward - and to date it has not been confirmed - the military sale would follow a signed agreement in 2013 to purchase a fleet of Tiger armored vehicles and an airborne flight simulator. In March this year, Foreign Minister Lavrov also offered to help provide security for the planned Nicaraguan canal, but that venture needs several years to be accomplished. Meantime, Russian financing for these projects is problematic given targeted U.S. sanctions on Russian banks which will make financial institution in Central America hesitant to enter joint ventures with Russian banks.

We may conclude from these visits and discussions over commercial sales that Russia wants to play a role in Central America. Previously, this region was considered a U.S. sphere of influence under the 19th century Monroe Doctrine, but globalization and the hemisphere's desire to diversify its trading links has resulted in a growing Russian and Chinese presence. Both seek markets for their heavy equipment and military industrial goods, as well as influence at the highest level of government. The Central American market for high valued aircraft and tanks is minimal, but the Russians have opened the door to explore opportunities.

What lies beyond commercial relations?

Since 2008, Russia has demonstrated that it can operate in the U.S. neighborhood. It has conducted military exercises in the Caribbean and sent naval assets to Nicaragua. The day before the U.S. delegation was due to start normalization talks in Havana, a Russian warship docked in Havana. The Meridian-class intelligence ship with a crew of approximately 200 had visited Havana in February and March 2014. The response from both U.S. and Cuban authorities was to play down the visit, treating it as ordinary. However, the timing this January sent the message that Russia should not be ignored; its government sought a role in Cuba's foreign policy.

Cuba is now publicly engaged on a major initiative with Washington. Russia has publicly endorsed this move and sees benefits from Cuban economic opening, as well as the development of an effective FDI regime. However, Russia has two explicit caveats: Cuba's sovereignty should not be infringed, i.e. the return of Guantanamo, and the trade embargo should be lifted. Given U.S. refusal to negotiate the transfer of Guantanamo and Congressional debate over the trade embargo, Russia may have to step back or the United States may find progress towards full normalization stalled. The degree of Raul Castro's independence from Moscow will be tested on these two issues.

---

[8] "Arms Deal with Nicaragua Boosts Russia's Presence in Latin America," Global Insights, May 2015
http://globalriskinsights.com/2015/05/arms-deal-with-nicaragua-boosts-russias-presence-in-latin-america/

Mr. DUNCAN. Well, thank all the panelists, great testimony. And now we will enter into the questioning phase and I will recognize myself for 5 minutes for questions.

First one, how does Russia cultivate ties with Latin American countries? Mr. Farah.

Mr. FARAH. It cultivates them largely through, as was mentioned numerous times, weapons sales and a constant stream of high profile visitors going through to give the impression that they care a great deal. You see the defense minister, you see the foreign minister, you see the head of counternarcotics, you see the head of Parliament, all parading through there multiple times a year. So, and they also offer a lot of things that aren't delivered, as I think Dr. Negroponte said. They create the illusion of doing more than what they do. But they also have an echo chamber that they have created with the ALBA nations particularly where that is never reported, and you hear the constant great things that the Russians are doing.

But I also think the more dangerous element, and I will be very brief on this, is the cultivation of much more significant intelligence ties and the providing of much more sophisticated intelligence apparatuses to the ALBA nations. You see it particularly in the newest member in El Salvador. You see a great deal of Russian equipment coming in. Nicaragua has it. Venezuela has it. Greatly increasing the power of the intelligence services which are geared entirely to monitoring their own people and suppressing dissent, and I think that is an incredibly dangerous but it is an enticing element.

And the reason they have some success in the weapons and other things is they attach no conditions. So if you are going to give them a lot of toys and no conditions, they would prefer that to getting issues from the United States where they may have to account for how they use those things.

Mr. DUNCAN. So in your opinion, Russia is getting something of value in return for their involvement? Are they getting what they want?

Mr. FARAH. I think that they wouldn't keep doing it if they weren't, sir. And I think that if you look at their, and I have a great deal in my testimony, particularly in the financial sector where they have made great inroads into the banking system to avoid international sanctions that the United States and the European Union have provided to them. I think that is very significant to their well-being. I think as others have mentioned, the ability to offload for some profit, aging arms systems that they can't really unload anyplace else but are useful in regions like Central America.

And as several other panelists have mentioned, friendship. They have a group of people who will support them against any charges in the United Nations and elsewhere, and whom they will protect. When Venezuela is up on human rights issues who is going to veto that in the Security Council? It is going to be Russia. They have culled to this a mutually beneficial relationship, yes.

Mr. DUNCAN. All right. Do you think Russia is seeking to provide political or military challenge to the United States in the Western Hemisphere? I will ask one of the others that. Dr. Rouvinski, do you think Russia is seeking to provide a political or military challenge to the United States in this hemisphere?

Mr. ROUVINSKI. I think Russia has pursued different interests if we take into consideration the period before the war in Georgia in 2008 and after the war. I think before the war, Russian interests in Latin America were mostly linked with the possibility to promote the interests of their Russian private and state enterprises. And we have seen actually the efforts not only directed toward the arms sales, but also to promote the interest of the Russian energy companies and oil companies in Latin America.

However, after the Georgian crisis of 2008, I think, following the support obtained by Russia from Nicaragua and Venezuela, Russia started to reevaluate its policy and objective in Latin America and started looking for more opportunities from that perspective. So I think definitely there are some signs that Russia is challenging the United States, building strong military ties with the group of countries that I was mentioning, Nicaragua, Venezuela and Cuba, though I would agree with Dr. Negroponte that Cuba seems to be much more cautious in dealing with Russia than Nicaragua was. Thank you.

Mr. DUNCAN. And just to kind of summarize what you said if I heard you correctly, early on since 2008 with Georgia, Russia basically said you meddle in my neighborhood, I am going to come over and meddle in your neighborhood. And is that sort of a simplified summation of what you are saying?

Mr. ROUVINSKI. I would agree with you. And also I think it is very important the recognition that what even by Nicaragua of the breakaway republics at present South Ossetia, because Russia was actually facing a great trouble in getting any recognition of those breakaway republics, and it seemed that Daniel Ortega offer of recognizing those republic came with no previous consultation. So I would agree it was a certain risk there on his behalf, but Nicaragua also quickly obtained some important benefits from Russia. Russia supplied some aid to Nicaragua in recognition of its support of the Russian state.

Mr. DUNCAN. I agree. From what I have learned about Nicaragua, it concerns me probably more than Venezuela here in October 2015.

Doug, we have seen all this naval activity and air space incursions, what do you think Russia is up to? Why do you think we are seeing them sail so close to our shores, come into the Gulf of Mexico, come close to our airspace both on the east coast and west coast? What do you think they are up to, in your opinion? Yes.

Mr. FARAH. I think they are very explicit if you read their own literature. And I was fortunate in a project I was doing to work with a Russian analyst who spoke both Russian and Spanish who was able to read a lot of their media and their papers, academic papers. They are very explicit, as I think Dr. Negroponte said, the idea they are very upset that we are, that they view the United States as in their backyard and they want to come in our backyard.

And they have this doctrine, the Gerasimov Doctrine, of creating this constant state of conflict in every sphere, not just military, economic and counternarcotics, all of these things. And if you see where they move into the region it is to directly challenge what the

United States does best and has been in the region for. That is why I think they put in the counternarcotics center.

I disagree a little bit with Dr. Negroponte in that it is a benefit to a lot of countries. It is primarily—I have been to the center there and the training is not of high quality at all and everybody acknowledges that. But what they do do is select out from there their best elements and take them back to Moscow and train them and then send them back into the region gaining access to a great deal of intelligence and operational capacity in the region.

So I think that there are multiple reasons that feed into their view that they need to be another superpower, regain their superpower status. And I think this doctrine, and it is fascinating because it is the basis of what Russia does all over the world and they are very explicit about it. This isn't some dark secret. They view conflict as a permanent state and we don't. We generally think if you overcome a certain conflict then you are in peace.

And this doctrine explicitly says you are going to be in constant conflict in an asymmetrical way until you are able to overcome the enemy, and you see that in a lot of what they do in Latin America. It is not military, but it is certainly in this sphere of the social media and the other media they control and the training they are giving and the recruitment they are doing is a very different type of thing.

Mr. DUNCAN. Well, my time is expired. The ranking member is younger than I am, but this really seems like a throwback to the Cold War and what we experienced when I was growing up with then, the Soviet Union and their incursion and probing and what not. So I will turn to the ranking member for 5 minutes.

Mr. SIRES. Chairman, you would be surprised how old I am. Dr. Negroponte, did I detect a sense that Russia is really more interested in markets than the military?

Ms. NEGROPONTE. Yes. Russia needs markets for its newly developed and sophisticated military equipment. It participates in military shows in Chile and in Peru in order to show what it has produced and for it not to be treated as some 1950 industrial base. So show is important, sales are important, and as of now, income is even more important.

Mr. SIRES. Thank you. Dr. Urcuyo, did you say that you felt that Americas are excessively in South America and Central America in the Western Hemisphere in your comments? And that is why the Russians——

Mr. URCUYO. Excessively what? Excuse me.

Mr. SIRES. That is the word you used because I wrote it down.

Mr. URCUYO. No, but I didn't follow your question.

Mr. SIRES. That you felt that the Americas were excessively in the Western Hemisphere and that is why

Russia——

Mr. URCUYO. No, no. Not at all. I think that the U.S. has been distracted in all the theaters of action and of war so you haven't been paying enough attention to what is happening in the Western Hemisphere. And suddenly you find out that there is vacuum, and that that vacuum has been occupied by China, economically speaking, and by Russia that tries to fill that vacuum. But I wouldn't be that dramatic.

And it may be I didn't explain myself in my first presentation, but I think that there is space for the strategic expansion of Russia but not in absolute terms.

Mr. SIRES. Because that is how I feel. I feel we haven't focused enough on the Western Hemisphere over the years, so when you said that it sort of struck a key in my head here. There is an awful lot of talk about how the Russians were so magnanimous and forgave Cuba its debt of $20 billion or whatever it was. First of all, Cuba could have never paid that debt.

Mr. URCUYO. Yes.

Mr. SIRES. So, I mean, this magnanimous effort by Russia, it really is nothing more than reality that Cuba can't pay whatever they owe Russia. So I would love to read that in the press how they play that up as something so big.

I have a comment here from SOUTHCOM Commander General Kelly. He has referred to the Russian's activity in Latin America as more of a nuisance as opposed to a threat, but has noted that the Russian presence underscores the importance of the United States remaining engaged with its partners in the region. Is it a nuisance or is it a threat? Dr. Negroponte?

Ms. NEGROPONTE. Ranking Member Sires, I believe that I support what General Kelly has said that it is a nuisance. There is so much hype, so much rhetoric, but when you come down to the real practical answer, who pays? Russia? Russian banks? They are not in a position to. Nicaragua? Nicaraguan banks? They are not in a position to. Cuba? The same. We have a term and a time of pragmatism in Cuba which does not permit Cuba to become a recipient of highly expensive equipment. So how did they pay for it?

Those restructuring of loans were undertaken in order to reduce the interest payments and then at the same time lease Ilyushin and Tupolev aircraft so-called to develop the tourist trade. I can understand Russians want to leave Russia in January, February and March, but the cost of those aircraft to carry tourists has been the reduced interest payments on those Cold War debts.

Mr. SIRES. Anybody else like to do that, whether it was a threat or——

Mr. URCUYO. Well, I was—in my original testimony there is a quote from a member of the Russian Academy of Sciences trying to explain where they are in Latin America at this moment and he says we are playing on Washington nerves. So for me, they are playing deliberately to irritate the region with their presence, but I will say there is a natural dramatic threat in this moment. But of course they are placing their dates and their points in the region looking for the median or long term, but I don't think that the immediate moment, an immediate term, Russia is a threat to the United States because of its activities in the Western Hemisphere. Maybe in the future, yes, taking into account this actual situation.

Mr. ROUVINSKI. Yes, I think we have to understand now what motivates Russia, do what Russia do with the military exercises, with the visits of the strategic bombers and with the navy.

Latin America, in the recent years transformed to be a very useful instrument for the Russian propaganda inside the country. More Russians worry about Latin America, and the image of Latin America I think it is quite different from reality. I have been living in Latin America and I had a chance to travel extensively. But because of this constructed image, Russian authorities are capable of taking advantage of these actions to show actually the capacity that perhaps not mesh exactly what Russia can do in real terms as a threat to the United States, but to show actually the Russian authority, Russian army is capable to mitigate the United States in the near abroad. So I think there is a great value for the Russian propaganda machine attached to what Russia is doing.

Mr. SIRES. My time—sorry, Mr. Farah, but my time has just expired.

Mr. DUNCAN. I want to thank the ranking member. Good line of questioning. I knew Cuba would be the thrust of your questioning and Russia's involvement there. I am going to go to the gentle lady who is now chair of the Middle East and North Africa Subcommittee and former chairman of the full committee, chairwoman of the full committee, Ms. Ileana Ros-Lehtinen.

Ms. ROS-LEHTINEN. Thank you so much, Mr. Chairman, Ranking Member. And thank you to my colleagues to my right. Thank you for bringing the spotlight on this expanding activities of Russia in our hemisphere. Putin's careful engagement seeks to create geopolitical allies in the region that support Russia's expansionist policies. It is not a coincidence that Argentina, Cuba, Nicaragua, Venezuela were some of the very few nations voting against the U.N. resolution declaring Crimea's independence referendum null and void.

The Russian Federation's activities in Latin America have a clear intent, eroding U.S. influence in our region, increasing military cooperation with the adversaries of democracy, of transparency, of the rule of law in Latin America. By forming military alliances and increasing defense cooperation, Russia has effectively gained power projection of forces right in our backyard.

According to the Russian defense minister, supersonic bombers are regularly patrolling the Caribbean Sea and the Gulf of Mexico to "monitor foreign military powers, military activities and maritime communications." And have on occasion made landings in Venezuela just as they did precisely 2 years ago today.

Earlier this year, a Russian intelligence vessel, as we know and you have talked about it, docked in Havana the day before the U.S.-Cuba talks were due to be held. And in testimony before the House Armed Services Committee, as Mr. Sires has pointed out, General John Kelly has asserted that the very same vessel has conducted operations in the Gulf of Mexico and the U.S. east coast. And we cannot forget that press reports from months ago stated that Russia intends to reopen the Lourdes spy facility in Cuba. We are hearing rumors that Cuban armed forces are helping to fight alongside Russian soldiers in Syria to come to the rescue of the murderous Assad regime.

But this provocation from Russia to seek to spy on our interests, to undermine our national security does not stop in Cuba. This year, Ortega agreed to allow Russia to establish a satellite station in Nicaragua, and Nicaragua recently expressed an interest in acquiring top of the line MiG-29 fighters to be used in counternarcotics operations, fueling fears that the Russians may have a continuous military footprint so close to our nation.

Russia has invested heavily in the development of Latin America, from the development of a nuclear plant in Argentina, Gazprom's gas ventures in Bolivia, technology transferred to the Nicaraguan Canal to the construction of a weapon factory in Venezuela. And the economic engagement, sir, which I read in your written testimony, Mr. Farah, has pointed out, in the past has opened the door for Russian organized crime to engage in new markets.

The Venezuelan regime, similarly, has a tradition of mixing business with criminal activities, and one example of this has been the Cartel de los Soles which had significant influence over senior officials in the Venezuelan regime. So I would ask you, sir, what impact, if any, has Russian organized crime had in the region, and are these groups working with organizations such as the Cartel de los Soles or perhaps the Mexican drug cartels? Thank you, Mr. Chairman.

Mr. DUNCAN. Mr. Farah.

Mr. FARAH. Thank you. I think that it is clear from what the Colombian law enforcement and intelligence communities are seeing in the Central Americas that there is a great deal of unaccounted for Russian shipping activity. I think that we don't pay a great deal of attention to it because it comes off the Pacific Coast of Central America and then goes to Russia. It doesn't come to the United States, so it is not something that we monitor very closely. But there are several new tuna fishing fleets who declare their primary market for tuna is Russia, which is economically irrational, and it is unlikely that they will be inspected as they come and go.

The Russians have very good access to Puerto Corinto into several ports. They just won the licitation for the port near San Miguel in El Salvador, where they are able to now come and go without much supervision. I think that the proximity of—the cocaine is produced largely the FARC and the FARC's ability to move the cocaine is largely dependent on the Cartel de los Soles. So if they are acquiring as they seem to be significant amounts of cocaine, it would have to be through that lineup. There is very little other way they could get significant amounts of cocaine out with impunity as the way they are doing.

And my understanding of the operation is that it largely goes to Nicaragua. It goes out Puerto Corinto. They have now opened up Puerto Corsain in El Salvador which is a government-controlled port, and they have free access there and they have declared it a military installation, although it is not a military installation. So no one can get in and out without permission of the President which is very difficult to acquire. So I think the contours are known, but I think that the details are something that require a lot more research.

Ms. ROS-LEHTINEN. Thank you very much, sir, and thank you, Mr. Chairman. Thank you to my colleagues.

Mr. DUNCAN. You are welcome. The chair will now go to Mr. Yoho from Florida.

Mr. YOHO. Thank you, Mr. Chairman. I appreciate the panel being here. Let's see here. Dr. Urcuyo, will Russia have more presence and influence in Cuba, Central and South America with the

Obama administration's attempt to relax sanctions in Cuba, in your opinion?

Mr. URCUYO. No, I don't think so. This has structural causes. First the inheritance of the past, for example, all the people that were trained by the USSR during the Central American wars. They are now in my—in the '60s and '50s. And, for example, we in Costa Rica have this guy that he went to the Frunze Military Academy, he graduated as a colonel, and he is part of the equivalent right now of the Communist Party of Costa Rica that has 70 years of existence.

Mr. YOHO. Okay, let me broaden my question and this will be for everybody. Do you see Russia having more presence in Cuba and Central and South America with the lack of response to Russia's invasion and annexation of Crimea, with no credible response from the U.S., or the red lines drawn by our administration in Syria on the use of chemical weapons, with no response from us once we found out those happened, calls for regime change and we did not act, and the Iran nuclear deal where we operated from a position of weakness and really got not a whole lot out of that but Iran got a whole lot? What is your opinion on those negotiations of those things I just laid out, allowing Russia to expand more? And we will start with Dr. Farah if we can, or Dr. Negroponte, you are ready. Go ahead.

Ms. NEGROPONTE. Thank you very much, Congressman Yoho. I think we must make clear distinctions between Russian expansionism in Central Europe, in Georgia and in Syria with its activities within the Western Hemisphere. The Western Hemisphere has traditionally been an area protected by the United States. Our distraction——

Mr. YOHO. That is going to lead to one of my other questions, so go ahead.

Ms. NEGROPONTE. Very good. Our distraction by events in the Middle East as serious as they are have taken us away from recognizing that the Western Hemisphere is our border. Travel to and from is plentiful and permanent. If we do not invest in interests in Central America, in developing our trade ties with South America, we should only expect that mischief makers will come to seek to take our place.

Mr. YOHO. Dr. Rouvinski.

Mr. ROUVINSKI. Thank you very much. I think in terms of Russian relations with Cuba it has been difficult for Russia to find a way to go back to the level of relationship in the 1990s when Cuba perceived Russia as a traitor, and abandoning of the Russian aid to Cuba actually caused a lot of trouble for the Russian political leaders. However, I think after the war with Georgia in 2008, Russia realized that because of the certain abandonment by the United States of Latin America it has a window of opportunities. And I think what they will do during that time and especially in the context of the crisis in Ukraine is actually a benefit on that possibilities that they have, and the forgiveness of the Cuban debt to Russia falls within this context.

Mr. YOHO. Mr. Farah.

Mr. FARAH. I think one has to distinguish between what the Russians gain at a state level with the ALBA nations particularly and what the popular perception, what people actually believe on the ground. So I think that the perception that the United States is not engaged is very widespread.

I think that while Russia is very engaged, and I think they are doing some dangerous things in the region, it is a very, I would say, shallow engagement. It is with the elites of regimes that—Ortega is very ill; he probably won't be around much longer. The Castro brothers can't live forever, one thing. Sanchez Ceren in El Salvador is very ill. And so you have a series of very personal relationships and past relationships that are allowing Russia to do a great deal now, but it is not that Russia is popular in the region or that people think that they would rather align on a macro level with Russia. It is a narrow and deep engagement with elites, and I think in very dangerous ways, but something that doesn't affect how people view the United States.

Mr. YOHO. Do you see a need to reinstate something like the Monroe Doctrine, since John Kerry said it was gone, it is no longer there? And I think that is a misstep on our foreign policy that we are just saying we yield, basically.

Mr. Chairman, I am over my time so I don't know how you want to handle that. Thank you.

Mr. DUNCAN. I thank the gentleman. I will now go to Mr. Byrne from Alabama.

Mr. BYRNE. Thank you, Mr. Chairman, and I appreciate being included in this very important hearing. I am a member of the House Armed Services Committee, not a member of this committee.

Dr. Rouvinski, I have just come back from your country, Colombia, had a 4-day trip with Congressman Gallego, and we learned that within the last year or so, Russian military aircraft had transited Colombian airspace without Colombian permission. First, is that your understanding as well, and if so who are the Russian sending a message to, the United States or Colombia, and what is that message?

Mr. ROUVINSKI. Yes, in fact, Russian strategic bombers, Tu-160, penetrated the Colombian airspace twice without the permission of the Colombian authorities. And the explanation that was given by Russia that the pilot did it by mistake, but they did it twice, and they flew from Venezuela to Nicaragua and from Nicaragua to Venezuela.

So in Colombia it was a very difficult situation for the Colombian Government to deal with it because it was widely perceived by the Colombian public that it was a message to support the Nicaragua stance in the territorial dispute between Colombia and Nicaragua over the San Andres Island in the Caribbean Sea. The Colombian Parliament had the special hearings on that respect, but finally they accepted the apology of the Russian side because I think Russians were not interested in jeopardizing their relation with Colombia. Colombia is very important for Russia because it does not belong to those groups of the country that are especially close with Russia.

So for Russia it is really a possibility to demonstrate that Russia can keep its diplomatic relationship not only with those country that ideologically are very close to Vladimir Putin, but also with Colombia. For example, this year Russian Minister of Foreign Affairs Lavrov paid a visit to Colombia to celebrate 18th anniversary of the establishment of the diplomatic relation between Colombia and Russia, and he met with President Santos and the minister of foreign affairs. So I think it is the explanation.

Mr. BYRNE. Thank you. Dr. Negroponte, I have a question for you about American relations with Cuba. I would say our country has made, or the President has made some unilateral efforts to upgrade the relationship between our two countries. There is a lot of suggestions that Congress should lift the trade embargo. We wonder about your view on that.

Should we request, or demand, before we lift the trade embargo that we have a clear understanding and agreement and forceful agreement with Cuba that they will not be a staging ground for foreign military actions or foreign intelligence actions against our country, and we will not be a staging ground against them? Do you think that is something we should require before we lift the trade embargo?

Ms. NEGROPONTE. Thank you, Congressman. I do not see it as a necessary part of the very tough negotiations that are taking place and will take place within this distinguished body over the lifting of the U.S. trade embargo. I think within the trade embargo, trade rules themselves, we have a number of very difficult issues and I am not sure that introducing the military element is necessarily going to aid either one side or the other.

However, I would note Foreign Minister Lavrov made it very clear in July this year that Russia welcomes the normalization of relations with the United States, that is Cuba and the United States, on two conditions. One is the sovereignty of Cuba, namely Guantanamo; and secondly is the lifting of the embargo. My reading of the discussions between the administration and the Cuban Government is that Guantanamo is not up for negotiation, and the issue of the embargo is an issue which this illustrious body will discuss, not Russia.

So that leaves Foreign Minister Lavrov and his boss to determine whether they are going to exert pressure on Raul Castro to concede, or whether Raul Castro has the ability to say thanks, Mr. Putin, this is an issue between Cuba and the United States and within the United States and the Congress of the United States, and would you please butt out. Thank you.

Mr. BYRNE. Mr. Farah, do you want to take a quick stab at that?

Mr. FARAH. It is not honestly my area of expertise, Congressman. I don't think it would be harmful to include the conditions as you laid them out of not being a foreign intelligence staging area and we agree not to do it to them. I don't think it is realistic to expect that any country in the region including that one would actually agree to that, so I am not sure that introducing that would bring— I don't find it unreasonable, but I don't think it is probably very realistic.

Mr. BYRNE. Thank you. Appreciate it, Mr. Chairman.

Mr. DUNCAN. I want to thank the gentleman. Not a member of the subcommittee, but a valuable member of our full committee and I appreciate his input.

And I am not a conspiracy theorist by nature, but I am a conspiracy theorist by nature. If you look at Google Earth and you go to the northeast corner of Nicaragua near the border of Costa Rica you are going to see an airbase that—airfield, rather—that is long enough to handle pretty much anything. It is in the middle of the jungle. It is near Lagoon, Ebo, and Spout Morris, close to the Costa Rican border, close to the Atlantic Ocean.

Why it was built, what it is there for, were the Russians involved, I was told they were. But anyway it is interesting to start thinking about the Russian presence in this hemisphere and delve into the questions that we have had today. The biggest question is why, why they are here, what can we do about it?

I think because there has been a vacuum of American engagement in this hemisphere over the past couple of decades, if not longer, that it provides an opportunity for Russia and China and others to come here. I think that is part of what we have been trying to investigate. I think if America gets more engaged with our friends and allies and neighbors here in the hemisphere we will all be better off and we will be able to thwart some of these incursions by Russia and others.

I don't have any other questions. I think the ranking member wanted to ask one more, so I am going to yield to him for as long as he needs. Thanks.

Mr. SIRES. Yes. I, just out of curiosity, just want to hear what you have to say. There are 30,000 Cubans in Venezuela. We have a government in Venezuela that is teetering on collapse. There is a lot of Russian effort to befriend Venezuela. Do you think that Russia would dare try to prop up another dictator in this region if the government collapses? I mean, they are building airfields here and there. I was just wondering, since I didn't get a chance to get your response before.

Mr. FARAH. Well, I think that the short answer, I think, is probably not in our hemisphere. I think that the Venezuelan regime has survived because of the Cuban intelligence apparatus has allowed it to maintain control in ways that it never would have been capable of on its own. I think that just as important to the regime survival has been China's willingness to buy everything with cash up front as they need cash, so that now half of Venezuelan's oil exports don't generate them any cash because they have already been paid for. So I think that there are a series of anomalous events that have allowed this regime to last as long as it can.

I would sincerely doubt because there is no other strategic interest for Russia in the region, and I would assume but you never know that that would be a bridge too far for them. And I think that that would force the United States to react in ways that they would have very difficult times maintaining supply lines and doing all the things that they would need to do, and I think that it would generate an enormous backlash in the region.

But I think that the presence of the Cubans and the Russians' willingness to engage with Venezuela and help them financially and with intelligence and with weapons is an important part of their ability to stay in power as long as they have.

Mr. ROUVINSKI. I think in terms of the possibility that Russians have an increased presence in Venezuela it is highly unlikely. We have seen during several crises in Venezuela that——

Mr. SIRES. Is that because Cuba has 30,000 people in Venezuela? I mean, they are basically doing the work for the Russians.

Mr. ROUVINSKI. Yes, I think the Russian presence in Venezuela has been because of the first place has stronger personal and sympathies and relations between some strong men in Russia and Venezuela, but I think there also have been some concern about Russian involvement there. I would agree with Mr. Farah that Venezuela is surviving, the Maduro regime is surviving because of the Chinese buying everything and because of the intelligence provided by Cuba. But Russian involvement, I really don't see that there will be more in recent terms.

Mr. SIRES. Dr. Urcuyo.

Mr. URCUYO. I agree with my colleagues in the sense that I think what props up Venezuela is the Chinese economic support and also the Cuban intelligence through the medics and doctors that are helping in the Misiones in Venezuela. But I don't think that the Russians will go boots on the ground in Venezuela or in any other country in Latin America.

Mr. SIRES. How about you, Dr. Negroponte?

Ms. NEGROPONTE. With the price of oil at under $50 a barrel, Russia's interest in Venezuela is minimal.

Mr. SIRES. Thanks. Thank you, Mr. Chairman.

Mr. DUNCAN. I want to thank the ranking member and I want to thank the members of the committee. And I thought this was a good hearing. I want to thank the panelists. I thought some very valuable insight to some of the issues well beyond what I expected. I want to thank the witnesses who traveled so far for making the time to come and inform Members of Congress so that we can make informed decisions going forward on good information.

We are going to keep the record open for 5 days. If members have additional questions, we will submit those to you. And with there being no further business for the committee, we will stand adjourned.

[Whereupon, at 3:10 p.m., the subcommittee adjourned.]

APPENDIX

Material Submitted for the Record

SUBCOMMITTEE HEARING NOTICE
COMMITTEE ON FOREIGN AFFAIRS
U.S. HOUSE OF REPRESENTATIVES
WASHINGTON, DC 20515-6128

Subcommittee on the Western Hemisphere
Jeff Duncan (R-SC), Chairman

TO: MEMBERS OF THE COMMITTEE ON FOREIGN AFFAIRS

You are respectfully requested to attend an OPEN hearing of the Committee on Foreign Affairs, to be held by the Subcommittee on the Western Hemisphere in *Room 2172 of the Rayburn House Office Building (and available live on the Committee website at http://www.ForeignAffairs.house.gov):

DATE: Thursday, October 22, 2015

TIME: 2:00 p.m.

SUBJECT: Russian Engagement in the Western Hemisphere

WITNESSES: Mr. Doug Farah
                   President
                   IBI Consultants

                   Vladimir Rouvinski, Ph.D.
                   Director of the CIES Interdisciplinary Research Center
                   Universidad Icesi in Colombia

                   Constantino Urcuyo, Ph.D.
                   Academic Director
                   Centro de Investigación y Adiestramiento Político Administrativo in Costa Rica

                   Mrs. Diana Villiers Negroponte
                   Public Policy Scholar
                   Woodrow Wilson International Center for Scholars

By Direction of the Chairman

COMMITTEE ON FOREIGN AFFAIRS

MINUTES OF SUBCOMMITTEE ON _____ *the Western Hemisphere* _____ HEARING

Day __*Thursday*__ Date __*October 22, 2015*__ Room _____ *2172* _____

Starting Time __*2:00 PM*__ Ending Time __*03:10 PM*__

Recesses _____ (____to____) (____to____) (____to____) (____to____) (____to____) (____to____)

Presiding Member(s)

Chairman Jeff Duncan

Check all of the following that apply:

Open Session ☑   Electronically Recorded (taped) ☑
Executive (closed) Session ☐   Stenographic Record ☑
Televised ☐

TITLE OF HEARING:

Russian Engagement in the Western Hemisphere

SUBCOMMITTEE MEMBERS PRESENT:

Chairman Jeff Duncan, Rep. Albio Sires, Rep. Ileana Ros-Lehtinen, Rep. Ted Yoho

NON-SUBCOMMITTEE MEMBERS PRESENT: *(Mark with an * if they are not members of full committee.)*

Rep. Bradley Byrne

HEARING WITNESSES: Same as meeting notice attached? Yes ☑ No ☐
(If "no", please list below and include title, agency, department, or organization.)

STATEMENTS FOR THE RECORD: *(List any statements submitted for the record.)*

N/A

TIME SCHEDULED TO RECONVENE _____
or
TIME ADJOURNED __*03:10 PM*__

Subcommittee Staff Director

MATERIAL SUBMITTED FOR THE RECORD BY THE HONORABLE ILEANA ROS-LEHTINEN,
A REPRESENTATIVE IN CONGRESS FROM THE STATE OF FLORIDA

Venezuela Awareness
Changing the Present...

November 6, 2015

Written Statement for the Record

Submitted by

Patricia Andrade

Venezuela Awareness Foundation

Human Rights Director

To

The Subcommittee on the Western Hemisphere

For the Subcommittee Hearing

"Deplorable Human Rights Violations in Cuba and Venezuela"

Venezuela Awareness Foundation thanks Chairman Mr. Jeff Duncan, Chairwoman Mrs. Ileana Ros-Lehtinen and other honorable members for holding this hearing. Venezuela Awareness respectfully wants to share with the members of the Committee, the deep concern about the damage caused by the contacts of the Counselor of the Department of State Thomas Shannon with senior representatives of the regime of Nicolas Maduro, giving them a facade of being "democratic" being a way to facilitate their perpetuation in power, having serious consequences by deepening human rights violations, persecution and political prisoners.

Venezuela Awareness mission is the defense of human rights and to denounce when they are violated for political reasons, monitoring the rapid deterioration and disappearance of civil liberties and fundamental rights as well as being the only voice since the violations began to be counted that has subsequently been mentioned in the annual human rights reports by the State Department, list that is updated and kept public.

In addition, we have responded to the needs of the Venezuelan political prisoners since the beginnings, revealing and denouncing the situations this group goes through such as the lack of guarantees for a fair trial, the lack of timely medical care that have put their lives at risk while in political imprisonment, torture and the convictions of innocent people only by order of the Executive, denouncing these violating situations in international bodies, NGOs, foreign governments, and the media.

Venezuela Awareness
Changing the Present...

Without justice there is no democracy, so the rules of the democratic game do not exist in Venezuela. That is why the issue of human rights became a priority on the agenda of Venezuela Awareness since the arrival of former President Hugo Chavez to power, a period where we could count about 500 political prisoners and once Nicolas Maduro assumes power in 2013, the number of political prisoners grew to about 4,000, remaining in political prison to this day 95 and about 20 are in house arrest condition.

We would like to call your attention to the situation facing the 95 political prisoners, emphasizing on the serious cases:

Of the group of political prisoners who are on the premises of the Bolivarian Intelligence Service (SEBIN) -The Helicoide in Caracas, 12 of them are suffering serious health problems that require urgent specialized care. According to international standards, people in custody by the State should receive sun every day. At the Helicoide theoretically they should receive sun twice a week, but rarely this is done, so political prisoners may spend seven months without receiving sun, with the aggravating that officials retaliate, excluding those they wish, taking away from them this privilege which in reality is a right. Additionally, to punish this group, sometimes they cut the water service to suspend the visits.

Most of the political prisoners at the SEBIN have not started their trials; they keep them incarcerated with the constant deferrals in the courts where their cases are held. If the regime wanted to release the political prisoners, they could had issued precautionary measures and continue their trial in freedom since all of them deserve their immediate release, their processes are flawed and all are innocent.

We take this opportunity to present cases of political prisoners who have extremely serious situations:

1.-Venezuelan political prisoners with longer political imprisonment; 12 years, six months and 18 days: Hector Rovain, Marco Hurtado, Luis Molina, Arube Perez and Erasmo Bolivar, who have serious health problems such as two of them have suffered heart attacks and the five should have been released, according to the law, eight years ago (in 2007), but the judge in the case, Ada Marina de Armas, refuses to release them due to their status as political prisoners.

2. Case of the retired captain Laided Salazar, who is in condition of isolation in the maximum security prison Fenix Uribana from May 5, 2014, in a cell of measures 3x2 meters with concrete bed and a bathroom where you can see the worms coming out of the toilet. When she entered political prison, Laided weighed 154 pounds and now she weighs 93 pounds. Thanks to a strong family pressure, after five months, on October 24 Laided was allowed to see her 11 years old son Rafaelito who spent two hours under the sun to be able to enter the prison and hug his mother. As a member of the military, the place of detention of the captain Laided Salazar should be the Ramo Verde military prison but to accentuate her punishment, this right is denied having to live with highly dangerous common prisoners.

Venezuela Awareness
changing the present...

3. Case of journalist Victor Garcia Hidalgo, who was released on a measure of house arrest in November 2013 for having serious health problems and since then, the permits to go to medical checkups are denied, so his health is deteriorating: blood pressure, problems with the retina because of a degenerative disease and he is losing his vision, spinal problems that require therapy among other problems.

4. University student Andrés León, detained on May 5, 2014 in Valencia, Carabobo State, tortured by the National Guard during his detention which required a lengthy hospitalization leaving him with serious health problems that threatened his life, so he was released on a humanitarian measure of house arrest last June 25, 2015, however, so far the transfer to his doctor to treat his serious ailments has been denied.

6. Victims of former Prosecutor Franklin Nieves, the young political prisoners, lawyers Rodrigo Jose and Jose Carlos Hernandez Diaz, incarcerated in the prison of Cumana, Sucre state, since April 18, 2013 because of the post-election protests that threatened to spread. Culprits were needed to intimidate the Venezuelans and thus stop the protests, so the photos of Rodrigo and Carlos Hernandez who were peacefully protesting outside their home in a gated community, were shown on television by Nicolas Maduro who asked the full weight of the law so the then National Prosecutor Franklin Nieves was commissioned who went to the city of Cumana to comply with Maduro's orders and thus produce false evidence, put together a case forging documents and thus control a political trial to get a condemning sentence with fabricated evidence. Thanks to former Prosecutor Franklin Nieves, Jose Carlos Hernandez was sentenced to 14 years and Rodrigo Jose Hernandez to 6 years and 6 months; they are serving their sentences in harsh conditions.

As the Hernandez brothers, dozens of protesting students in 2014 were accused of serious crimes with evidence fabricated by the then Prosecutor Nieves who knew the students were innocent and they were only exercising their constitutional right to peaceful protest.

Venezuela Awareness wishes to state that former Prosecutor Franklin Nieves, who for several days has been in Miami requesting asylum without being politically persecuted, was denounced in the US for his actions violating human rights during the protests of 2014, so we cannot understand why a person that has been for over a decade, one of the worst violators of human rights during the Chavista process, is in the US territory where victims of the former prosecutor are.

We insist that the stay of the former Prosecutor Nieves in America is a mockery of the "Venezuela Defense of Human Rights and Civil Society Act of 2014" passed in the US Congress, as it was created to sanction human rights violators during the protests of 2014 such as the former National Prosecutor Franklin Nieves who was one of the most active because he had the full confidence of the Attorney General Luisa Ortega Diaz.

Venezuela Awareness
Changing the Present...

Additionally, Nieves represents the mockery of the search for justice for the victims, living the golden exile with money of unknown origins and he manages a media platform that draws attention because of the high cost of it for somebody who says he does not have money to justify his new way of life in Miami, so we ask for him to be investigated.

Finally, we would like to add that on November 4, 2015, the former prosecutor Nieves made serious accusations against this organization in the news agency EFE because of our work on human rights, that is to say, he repeats his behavior of Venezuela of falsely accusing, of attacking human rights defenders, and more serious, he pretends to deny his doing in other cases using Leopoldo Lopez as a shield to victimize himself and to manufacture, as it is his experience, a fraudulent asylum. Is this the kind of person who deserves to live in America when he does not show the slightest respect for his victims, the persecuted because of political reasons, US citizens and human rights defenders?

In the coming days we will publish serious cases of human rights violations of the former Prosecutor Nieves hoping that justice be made and he is requested to abandon the US territory because he is one of the named to be sanctioned by the " Venezuela Defense of Human Rights and Civil Society Act of 2014" and because his presence poses a threat to their victims who took refuge in this great nation.

Venezuela Awareness trust in your good offices to ease the pain of the 95 Venezuelan political prisoners so they can return home, those who remain under house arrest to have access to specialized medical care and their full freedom; and finally, we respectfully request your support to not allowing the former Prosecutor Nieves to remain on US soil for having committed serious violations of human rights for more than a decade.

Thank you for your consideration of our recommendations.

Patricia Andrade
Venezuelan Awareness
Human Rights Director